Texas Death Row Yogi

Spiritual Confessions of a Death Row Inmate

Written by
Pete Russell

©2013, Pete Russell, Livingston, Texas.

ISBN: 978-1-300-31778-4

Second edition.

Edited and designed by Pete Russell.

Texas Death Row, 2013. This is the spiritual autobiography of a Texas Death Row inmate and his journey to seek liberation within himself. In this book, Pete compiles and compares the writings of different systems of belief to show us how they are all sending us the same message , that "love" is the answer.

Dedications

To my lovely mother, Jevenia Russell who has always stood by my side in good and bad times, regardless of the circumstances. I love you, Mama and thank you.

To my beloved Guru, spiritual teacher and guide, Swami Chidvilasananda, the supreme Siddha and the bestower of grace. And to the divine Masters of the Siddha lineage, Swami Muktananda and Bhagavan Nityananda. I bow to your feet.

Table of Contents

Dedications..5

Table of Contents...6

Introduction...8

Author's Note...12

Chapter 1 Meditation..21

Chapter 2 The Mind and Senses..........................28

Chapter 3 The Knowledge of Self.........................33

Chapter 4 The Knowledge of the Soul..................37

Chapter 5 The God Within...................................39

Chapter 6 An Interview with Pete........................42

Chapter 7 The Precepts of the Gurus...................53

Chapter 8 The Origin of Confusion......................61

Chapter 10 Shaktipat Diksha...............................70

Chapter 11 My Experience of Shaktipat Diksha Initiation............76

Chapter 12 The Chakras.......................................82

Chapter 13 Ezekiel's Wheel.................................91

Chapter 14 The Samskaras...................................97

Chapter 15 Karma and Reincarnation.................104

Chapter 16 What is Death?.................................111

Chapter 17 The Yoga of Jesus, Part 1.................116

Chapter 18 The Yoga of Jesus, Part 2.................123

Chapter 19 The Yoga of Jesus, Part 3.................133

Chapter 20 The Reality of God..138

Chapter 21 The Crucifixion and Resurrection of the Soul..............148

Chapter 22 The Origin of the Ego...154

Chapter 23 The Four Gatekeepers...160

Chapter 24 Yogic Diet..166

Chapter 25 Yogic Exercise for the Mind, Body and Spirit.............172

Chapter 26 Yogic Thinking...176

Chapter 27 *Pranayama*..182

Afterword..189

Acknowledgements..192

Source Notes...194

Introduction

I met Pete Russell a few years ago through our mutual practice of the spiritual path known as Siddha Yoga. I had known other Texas Death Row inmates who also practiced Siddha Yoga and I had visited them as well, up to their dates of execution. I was with them for that event, too.

The first time I met Pete, I was on a tour of prisons in Texas and Louisiana with another Siddha Yoga devotee. Pete had told us that he had stayed awake all night in anticipation of our visit. I remember that his eyes were positively lit up and he asked many questions about our path. There were words he didn't know how to pronounce because he had never heard them out loud. And chants that he wanted to learn but wasn't allowed to listen to. So we sat together for two hours and gave him as many answers as we could and sang the chants that he had never heard before.

Since then, I've gone several times on my own to visit Pete. Pete is a person who is completely positive. He always has a big smile on his face. It's as if he is as happy living on death row as I am living in the outside world. I know this cannot be true, but I also know that Pete will find a way to make prison a paradise and show others the way as well. He never complains to me and is always happy to tell me about the spiritual experiences he is having in meditation. I am amazed to hear about his spiritual life. Pete has accomplished more in just a few years spiritually than most people do in a lifetime.

Pete lives a life of spiritual investigation. He maintains a daily practice of meditation and chanting, two of the main practices on the Siddha Yoga path. During meditation, he focuses on the divine presence within and he has experienced his own divinity as you will come to understand in this book. And when he is finished with his daily practices, he reads spiritual texts from all religions. He is committed to finding the truth present in all systems of belief and this book is the result of that search.

It's a blessing in my life to know Pete. He is a great Siddha yogi and I am pleased to call him my friend. When he asked me to type and edit this book over a year ago, I agreed because I felt that Pete has something important to share with the world. The information in the book is important, but throughout the book you will receive something even more important. You will receive the great state of someone who has devoted each day to knowing God. The energy of his devotional practices is present in every page.

Thank you Pete, for being a great example to others of what can be accomplished when one focuses with great devotion on their own inner Light. You are a rare gift in this world.

Julie Muller
Houston, Texas

Author's Note

I was born on May 2, 1973 in Houston, Texas. I was told that my mother was the happiest woman in the world because she had given birth to a healthy baby boy. I was the first child and was named after my father. At that time, my father was in the military and we later learned that he abandoned my mother and me to marry another woman.

I was raised by my mother and my grandmother. When mother was working nights, I would spend the night at my grandmother's house. Our neighborhood in Houston was known as the Fifth Ward, but those of us who lived there knew it as "the bloody Fifth". At that time, it was one of the most violent neighborhoods in Houston. I saw every crime under the sun right in my own neighborhood.

At an early age, I understood that we were poor and struggling. We accepted everything the government had to give us with a smile. I remember standing in long lines with my mother to receive government food - cheese, butter, syrup, beans, rice and peanut butter.

In elementary school, we were subjected to "pops" or what they call now corporal punishment. If I suspected that I might get "popped" I would leave school and run home.

In middle school, I was sent to a vocational school so that I could learn a trade. This was in 1988. Although I was successful in that school, I was already selling drugs. Like most of my friends, we all wanted to wear the designer clothes our parents couldn't afford and selling drugs was the only way to get what we thought we had to have. I was just another punk with no future.

In 1991, I was charged with assault with a deadly weapon and aggravated robbery. I was sentenced to eight years in prison and didn't come home until 1999. While I was there, I earned my high school diploma, but I also lived in a dangerous, drug-infested world with men who, like me, thought that the only way up was through a world of crime.

I honestly made an effort to go straight when I finally got out. I worked at MacDonald's, washed cars, did landscaping - all the time hoping for something better. I got little support from my family and when I saw no future for myself, I began selling drugs again.

In 2001, I was busted for selling crack cocaine and arrested on my birthday (happy birthday!). In August, I was sentenced to 10 more years in prison. I was allowed to go home and get my affairs in order before reporting to begin serving my sentence. Three days later, I was charged with the murder of my girlfriend. So there was no 10 year sentence for me - the Texas jury that tried me sentenced me to death by execution on Death Row.

I arrived at Death Row in *Living*ston, Texas and very quickly saw the harsh environment that was so much worse than anything I could have imagined. The prison guards wanted to break me in, so I was deprived of food several times in those first days until I understood what the guards expected of me.

There was no orientation to Death Row - only ruthless commands that I didn't always understand. The food here is horrible and has not improved over the years.

The inmate in the cell next to me offered me some stamps so that I could write and let my family know my cell number and where to write me. It was the first act of kindness I'd known in a long time.

I began to write my mother. At this point, Mom was old and in poor health. I can't imagine what it is like for her to have her eldest son on Death Row. I put on a brave face, wrote to her that I was just fine and that all was in good order.

The size of my death row home is a cell that measures about 7'x10' and I have a mattress, a small writing table, a sink and toilet. No one ever touches me. I wear handcuffs whenever I leave my cell except for one hour a day, when I am allowed to go to a larger cage with other inmates to walk around. The other 23 hours, I spend in my cell. We're allowed to have a small radio and this is a link to the outside world. I'm allowed to have one visit per week , for two hours each, but many weeks go by without a visit.

On that first day, I was taken to a cage where the inmates are on "death watch". Those are the ones with an execution date or who are new and may try to commit suicide. In fact, I was approached by an inmate "J-real" who was facing execution that very day. It was my first day and it was his last. On his last day, he told me about creating my own life with God and not letting the environment dictate to me who I am and who I will become. After I arrived back in my cell, I sat and cried for the first time in a long time.

Around 6:15 p.m. that evening, I noticed it was quiet - too quiet. I began to look out of my cell to see what was going on. Apparently, most of the inmates were listening on their radios to see if J-real might get a stay of execution. But that was not to be and someone yelled out finally, "They got him".

It hit home to me where I was - in a place where people are treated like animals. "Respect" is not a word used in regards to our treatment, so we try to treat each other with decency. It's been years since I've had a hug or been embraced by anyone. I've not been patted on the back or told I did a good job at something, because the truth is, there is no occupation here for us who would like to do a good job. We're kept in tiny cells for 23 hours a day. We are allowed one visit per week for two hours, but my family has long since realized that the pain of coming to see me just isn't worth it. Occasionally, I receive a visit from a Christian woman who regularly visits the inmates and I get very rare visits from an attorney who seems disinterested in whether I'll live or die here. I'm viewed as a monster and a burden by society and a threat by the guards. My friends disappear one by one, as their dates for execution come up. We know whose turn it is and we try to stand strong for our brothers who go before us to meet their fate.

My life wasn't always like this. I didn't come into this world a criminal. I was as innocent as any other child. My great-grandmother was a Sunday school teacher and

I was taught the many stories of the Bible growing up. I loved them and I wanted an experience of God like those that were described in the Bible. I wanted the skies to open up and to hear the voice of God speaking to me. I loved the book of Revelations but at my church it was never mentioned. I began asking questions that no one seemed able or willing to answer. As hard as my life was, I believed in God and longed for a true relationship with him.

Once on Death Row, I realized that more than ever, I would need to make something out of myself. I know that sounds crazy in an environment where no one can become anyone of importance in the outside world. But I knew that if I were to survive, I would have to become more than what I had been in my past.

While in prison, serving my eight year sentence, I began to study Islam, which wasn't welcome news to my very Christian family. I was allowed to attend a Muslim worship service once a week where I met other African American brothers who were seekers like me. One brother in particular began to teach me all about the Islamic faith and also began to open up my mind to other esoteric religions. I asked many questions during those services and they patiently answered as well as they could.

I began to open up in a way I had never done before. My understanding of what it meant to live a spiritual life began to unfold. I was praying in Arabic five times a day and fasting according to the tradition during the time of Ramadan. At that time I was studying both the Qur'an and the Christian Bible. I saw inspiration in both. As I continued to dive deeper into my spiritual life, I found that I still had a vacant spot within me, something that was out of my grasp that I was reaching for. But I had no idea who or what it was I was reaching for.

During the month of Ramadan, a book of Indian scriptures came to me called the *Upanishads*. I began to read it and it had a strong impression on me. This book stated that Man draws near to God through direct experience. That's what I wanted, even as a child, to have a direct experience of God. That night when I closed my eyes I had a profound experience within that I can only describe as a "whoosh" going through my body. I sat up scared, and made sure I wasn't dreaming. I had no idea what was happening, but I knew it was powerful and was related to the scriptures I had been reading.

Once again, I lay back down and the experience came again, stronger this time. My breath became still and I was travelling fast in a white-bluish light. I saw the heavens - stars, the moon and sun. All this I witnessed within a profound feeling of peace. It was a peace I never wanted to come back from.

The next day, I gave someone else the book to read and he ecstatically told me later that he had had the same mystical experience. After searching for so long, I had finally had a direct experience of God. I understood the immense possibilities of living a life seeking that divine connection within myself. I felt that my boyhood dream was answered and that I was now earnestly on my spiritual path. So many great spiritual experiences have come to me since that initial experience, and my humble understanding has produced this book.

I hope that you find that relationship with God that brings you love, inner peace and the contentment that we all long for. Namaste.

Pete Russell
Texas Death Row, 2012

Chapter 1 - Meditation

Look within...meditate...you will find your own peace...you will find your own treasure.

-Gurumayi Chidvilasananda

Some perceive (experience) the Self within through meditation.

-The Bhagavad Gita

I believe meditation is the only medicine for the mind. This is my motto. Why do I say that? If you could see the mental state here on Texas Death Row, then you would agree with me that meditation is the only medicine.

There are several psychologists that walk around Death Row speaking to inmates about their mental state. I ask one lady, "Why don't they teach meditation to the inmates?" She said, "They won't let us". I said, "Who are they?" She said, "You know". I began to explain to her the benefits of meditation and that if meditation was taught on Death Row, a lot of the self-mutilation and disrespect between inmates and officers would stop. She agreed with me and walked away.

This leads us to our first question. What is meditation? According to Swami Muktananda, "Meditation is true prayer. True prayer is absorption in the Lord, and that is what meditation is."

We should all be familiar with prayer. Most of us were raised in church or had parents that taught us how to pray. Meditation is true prayer. There is nothing strange or foreign about it. Prayer and meditation have been around since the beginning of time and can be found in all religions of the world. Even Jesus taught his disciples how to pray. Jesus said:

"But thou, when thou prayest, enter into thy closet (the silence within) and when thou hast shut thy door (withdrawn the mind from the senses) pray to the Father which is in secret (in the inner transcendent divine consciousness) and thy Father which seeth in secret shall reward thee openly (shall bless you with the ever new bliss of his being)."

We should all have the understanding of prayer. Your closet is your heart; God lives within your heart. When we enter the heart, we enter the presence of God. This is when the absorption takes place, also known as the *samadhi* state. The *Svetasvatara Upanishad* says:

"When one knows God who is hidden in the heart of all things, even as cream is hidden in milk, and in whose glory all things are, he is free from all bondage."

It really would be nice to see inmates meditating throughout the prison system, and especially on Death Row. Meditation is the way. Don't worry if your friends or homeboys laugh or make fun of you. It's okay; in the end they will be meditating too. We are all on the path to God, whether we consciously realize it or not. So my brothers here on Death Row notice my state and ask me questions about God and meditation. No matter how tough one is on the outside, we all want to feel inner peace.

So people complain that they can't meditate and this is due to the restlessness of the mind. A person that has a restless mind is out of control, agitated, and always aggravated. Swami Muktananda says:

"When your mind is restless and turbulent, when you think negatively all the time, you harm not only yourself, but others as well."

You can see this in prison with all the fighting, and in the world with all the wars. It is obvious we have a problem, but no one has come up with a solid solution. The madness that you see is only a reflection of man's mind. There will never be peace until man makes peace with himself. This is why we must turn within and meditate.

There are several *Upanishads* that give instructions on how to meditate. The *Svetasvatara Upanishad* says:

" *Holding one's body steady with the three upper parts in a line (that is, with the back straight) and bringing the senses and the mind into the heart, a wise person should cross over all of the rivers of anxiety with the boat of the holy power (Brahman). Having controlled one's breathing here (in the body), let one restrain the mind without distraction, the way a chariot is yoked to wild horses.*"

The *Yoga Sikha Upanishad* says:

"Choosing a posture such as the lotus position, or whatever else may please him. Controlling the mind at all times, the wise should meditate continuously on the syllable Aum (OM) enthroning the highest God in their hearts."

In Siddha Yoga Meditation, we are taught to meditate on our divine Self. By meditating on our Self (the inner Self) we become one with the Self. This is the highest form of meditation. The Guru is the Self as well as God...meditate! In order to hold on to God, you must let go of all you worries. The mind must be stilled, so that you can look God face-to-face, see God with your third eye, located between the eye brows.

Swami Muktananda says: "The meditator should merge all his senses into the one Self and become completely absorbed in it. He should become completely absorbed in it. He should meditate on Shiva seeing the same one in all different thoughts and objects and lose himself in this meditation. Thus he will realize Brahman." This is called Siddha Meditation.

Anyone can meditate. Do you believe that? Start by finding a quiet place to sit and make a practice of sitting quietly in that same place for a few minutes every day. You can use the aid of the mantra, which I will explain later in this book, or you can use a powerful mantra from your own religion. It should be uplifting and positive. Don't be discouraged if the mind doesn't want to settle down at first. It's had its own way with you for years and years!

Continue to offer the mantra and be patient with the process. It will yield fruit! Be consistent and let meditation slowly but surely begin to change your life.

Questions for personal study:
1. What does meditation mean to you?
2. How often do you practice meditation?
3. How long do you meditate?
4. Do you have a special place in your house where you meditate?
5. What do you mediatate on?

Chapter 2 The Mind and Senses

"When the five senses and the mind are still and reason itself rests in silence, then begins the path supreme. This calm steadiness of the senses is called Yoga."

-*Katha Upanishad*

I have been on Texas Death Row for over seven years and in that time; I have practiced the teachings of Siddha Yoga Meditation. Through my practices, I have learned a great deal about the mind and how it works. I have come to the conclusion that, without a proper understanding of the mind, Man will continue to suffer. Not only will he continue to suffer but, out of ignorance, he will continue to hurt his brothers.

Here on Death Row the conditions are worsening every day. I have witnessed first-hand the mental breakdown of inmates: the crying, the screaming, the self-mutilation, setting fires and throwing urine and feces on each other. This breakdown is called "Death Row syndrome", and it is the leading cause of inmates dropping their appeals and committing suicide. This syndrome is a psychosis of the mind. The American Heritage Dictionary defines *psychosis* as a severe mental disorder.

How do we overcome this psychosis? By having a thorough understanding of the mind and senses. The American Heritage Dictionary defines *mind* as follows: The human consciousness that originates in the brain and is manifested especially in thought, perception, feeling, will, memory, or imagination.

In the Hindu scriptures, there are four functions of the mind and they are: *manas, buddhi, chitta* and *ahamkara.*

1. *Manas*: When the mind is filled with thoughts, this part of the mind is called *manas.* Mental activity that perceives, imagines, desires, doubts, and collects sense impressions. By itself, it cannot evaluate, decide or make judgments about these perceptions.

2. *Buddhi* or intellect: Makes decisions. It contains the ability to discriminate, judge, and classify the information perceived or created by *manas.*

3. *Chitta:* or subconscious mind. Remembers and files away every thought and action that we

experience, creating a vast reservoir of impressions or samskaras, which arise as memories.

4. *Ahamkara* or ego: Interprets everything in terms of I, me and mine. By the accumulation of life's experiences, the ego creates our sense of individuality and separateness, the limited or impure Self.

The scriptures say that the mind follows the pull of the senses. Through the senses the individual soul is able to experience the world and all its objects. The objects stimulate the senses which create likes and dislikes. In the *Katha Upanishad* it says:

"The Creator made the senses outward-going: They go to the world of matter outside, not to the Spirit within."

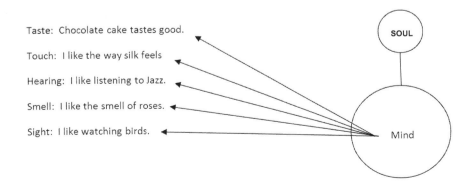

Taste: Chocolate cake tastes good.

Touch: I like the way silk feels

Hearing: I like listening to Jazz.

Smell: I like the smell of roses.

Sight: I like watching birds.

SOUL

Mind

The scriptures also say, "When the Soul becomes one with the mind and the senses, he is called one who has joys and sorrows. So, likes and dislikes are the very cause of pain and pleasure. In the *Katha Upanishad*, it says:

"He who has not right understanding (wrong knowledge) and whose mind is never steady (restless) is not the ruler (controller) of his life, like a bad driver with wild horses."

Now that we have an understanding of the mind and senses, we can apply the cure for the psychosis. That cure is meditation. In the Bible, Paul says, "Be ye transformed by the renewing of your mind." Paul is telling us that in order to make any type of psychological adjustment, one has to understand that everything is mental, and with this understanding, the transformation becomes easier.

If we are looking to change for the better, then we have to take control of our mind. The renewing of the mind is meditation in that it restores and revives the mind to its proper state which is pure consciousness. This consciousness is called *chiti* and represents the creative aspect of God. The transformation takes place when the mind and senses are completely still. This stillness allows us to see and feel God's presence within as divine consciousness. In the Bible, Psalms 46:10, it says: "Be still and know (have a direct experience) that I am God", meaning that only through stillness of the mind can we know God.

Sometimes I sit in my cell and I hear other inmates screaming or crying out in emotional pain. I hear the sounds of desperation and deeply-felt despair. In meditation, I can see that these are all manifestations of a profound longing to experience God and to feel his love. People call out and reach out looking for God. But God dwells in the most difficult place to go, deep within your own being. Meditation is the key to unlock this great mystery. In meditation we make the great discovery described by Swami Muktananda - " God dwells within you as you".

Questions for personal study:
1. What is the mind and senses?
2. Can you control your mind and senses?
3. How does the soul experience the world?
4. What is the best way to control the mind?
5. How can we renew our mind and senses?

Chapter 3 The Knowledge of Self

"When awake to the vision of the Atman, our own Self, when a man in truth can say I am He, what desires could lead him to grieve in fear for the body?"

-The Supreme Teaching

For thousands of years the wise sages and prophets have repeatedly asked man to wake up, into the knowledge of the Self. That is to say, to become conscious of your true divine Self and realize that God dwells within you as you.

The knowledge of Self is supreme knowledge. It is the knowledge of knowing that the inner Self (God) dwells in man. This knowledge is the foundation of all things in existence. Knowledge is God and God is all-knowing. God is the all in All, and all things were created by God, and have become God.

The *Svetasvatara Upanishad* says, "He is God, hidden in all beings, their inmost Soul who is in All. He watches the works of Creation, lives in all things, watches all things".

The purpose of life here on Earth is self-realization. Self-realization is the process of understanding the soul to be different from the body. Unfortunately, man has forgot the reason why he's here, and so he eats, drinks, and sleeps only to repeat the cycle of birth, death and rebirth. A wise poet has said:

"Wake up at least now, o thou careless one. Why waste thy love on a world that is transient? O Man, wake up, o wake up. Get away from this illusive net of *maya*. O Man, wake up, o wake up."

This poet is saying to become aware of that which will pass away and crumble into dust. Those things are worthless to dwell on, yet we constantly think about the temporary things of life.

The *Svetasvatara Upanishad* says: "When a man knows God, he is free. His sorrows have an end, and birth and death are no more."

As man began to inquire more about his Self, three questions will arise that he should contemplate very deeply. *Who am I? Why am I here?* and *Where am I going?* This is called self-inquiry. Understand that when these questions are properly answered, they will unlock the mysteries of heaven and bring man closer to the experience of the Self within. It would be wise for you to repeat these questions several times to yourself verbally and mentally. I will give my own answers to each question from my own contemplations. The answers to these questions change as you grow in spiritual wisdom.

1. Who am I? I am spirit and Soul. I was made in the divine image and likeness of God. I am not this body! I am an individual soul dwelling within this body.

2. Why am I here? To experience the fruit of my karma. I am a spiritual being having a physical experience here on earth, because of my karma. I understand that man reaps what he sows.

3. Where am I going? Back to God. The Prasna Upanishad says: Even as birds, of the Beloved, return to their tree for rest, thus all things find their rest in Atman, the supreme Spirit.

By meditating on these questions every day, you will see that the answers are to be experienced within. You may think that these questions don't interest you, but I ask you to think about it. What causes you to run after money, cars and powerful friends? Deep down, you are trying to answer the question *Who am I?* When something that you wanted turns out to be something that you don't want anymore, you are answering the question of *Where am I going?* And when you think about making changes in your life you are really pondering the question of *Why am I here?* Believe it or not, we live with these questions throughout our lives and when we consciously seek to answer these questions, our real spiritual journey begins.

Questions for personal study:

1. What is the highest knowledge?
2. When a person says he has self-knowledge, what is he saying?
3. As human beings, what is our purpose here on Earth?
4. What are the three questions Man should ask himself?
5. In your own life, what actions can you take to begin to find the answers to these questions?

Chapter 4 The Knowledge of the Soul

"And by the soul and he who perfected it"
- *The Qur'ran*

" The individual Soul was created in the image and likeness of God. The Soul in its purest form is a perfect reflection of God. In the Svetasvatara Upanishad it states:

The Soul is like the sun in Splendor. When it becomes one with the self-conscious "I am" and its desires, it is a flame the size of a thumb, but when one develops pure reason and the inner spirit, it becomes in concentration as the point of a needle.

The soul can be thought of as the part of a point of a hair which divided by a hundred was divided by a hundred again. And yet, in this living soul, there is the seed of infinity.

The Soul is not a man, nor a woman, nor what is neither a woman nor a man. When the Soul takes the form of a body, by that same body, the soul is bound.

The Soul is born and unfolds in a body, with dreams and desires and the food of life. And then it is reborn in new bodies, in accordance with its former works.

The Soul is also known as the jiva or the little self, Self-knowledge is soul knowledge. It is the only knowledge that will free you from identification with the body."

Within each human life, there is the potential to know God and to know your own divine Self. As your meditation develops, your inner vision becomes more and more in tune with your own divine nature. The Soul is bound to the body because of the good and bad actions of Man. Once Man turns his mind inwards towards God, the spell of illusion is broken and the Soul will soon be free of the body and the cycle of birth and death will be broken.

Questions for personal study:
1. The soul is created in the ___ and ___ of God.
2. Why does the soul reflect God?
3. Is the soul a man or a woman?
4. The soul is also known as ___
5. The soul will be free when ___

Chapter 5 The God Within

"For God is not the author of confusion, but of peace, as in all the churches of the saints."
-*The Bible*

If God is not the author of confusion, then what happens to man? If man comes from God, then why is he confused about God? There have been a lot of heated debates on whom or what God is, and how the universe was created. These debates, mostly politically motivated, opened the doors for the Crusades and the Inquisition in which millions of people lost their lives. In this day, we have terrorists acting in the name of their God. And lives continue to be lost in the name of God.

Every day, you can still hear and see people debating about God in church, the schools, and even the courtroom. Some people believe in the big bang theory, others believe in evolution and there are some people who don't believe in God at all. Debating about my god and your god, the right to kill each other if my God isn't your God, only shows that man is truly confused and unconscious to the knowledge of the Self. That is, he is unconscious that the very

God he is debating about is present and waiting for him within his heart. Jesus said, "Blessed are the pure (conscious) in heart for they shall see (experience) God." If man's heart was pure, there would be no need to debate about God. He would be able to see God within his own self and creation. And he would be able to see and witness God in others. In Jnaneshwar's *Commentary on the Bhagavad Gita*, Lord Krishna says, "If you purify your mind with thoughts of the Lord, with contemplation of the Lord, with repetition of the name of the Lord, you discover a new creation of the Lord within yourself."

In the words of Swami Muktananda, "If a mirror is dirty, it cannot reflect objects clearly. In the same way, a mind that has become dirty by association with outer objects cannot reflect the inner consciousness. But if it is cleaned by the practice of spiritual discipline, you can see the Self reflected in it."

Look within your own heart. Question your own motives. Do you do things only for yourself, or do you think about what's best for everyone when you make a decision? Constantly watch the mind, for the thoughts of the mind are connected to the purity of the heart.

Questions for personal study:

1. Why do people kill in the name of God?
2. What does it mean for you to have a pure heart?
3. Think of examples in your life that prove that you are "pure in heart".
4. Think of some examples of maya (illusion) in your life.
5. Where is the temple of God?

Chapter 6 An Interview with Pete

When did you learn about yoga for the first time? And how did you start to practice it?

I first learned about yoga when I came to Death Row. My neighbor was cleaning his cell and he threw away a lot of books. Some of the books were in good condition; others were badly torn. I had just arrived on Death Row and I didn't have anything to read. So I asked a guard to hand me one of the books on the floor. He kicked several books to my cell so that I could stick my hand out and get them. I'll never forget I picked up this book called *Mukteshwari* and started to read, "Oneness: The world is God". The teachings in this book were powerful. I wanted to learn more. There was an address in the back of the book offering free meditation courses. I signed up and that's how I started practicing Siddha Yoga Meditation.

How long have you practiced Yoga? Can you describe the transition you have experienced through years of practicing?

I have practiced Siddha Yoga for 5 ½ years. My transition is an ongoing process of spiritual growth and development. This is why meditation is so important. Man is what he thinks he is. If all the incarcerated individuals here can all meditate on love and peace then love and peace will begin to flow throughout Death Row, touching the hearts and minds of inmates and officers. So my experience is one of love, even in the midst of the Death Row syndrome. Think love, be love; that's the formula.

How have you maintained your sanity and health despite the extremely difficult and harsh confinement of Death Row?

This is a good question that deserves a good answer. There are studies that show that Death Row inmates are suffering from a type of syndrome, a psychological disorder that has plagued the entire Death Row population. Swami Muktananda said, "Mental disease is nothing but the state of mind whose thoughts have gone out of control". However, I maintain my sanity and health by practicing Siddha Yoga Meditation. I meditate on my higher Self (Shiva, the inner bliss). In this way I am able to rise above or tune out the syndrome that is mentally affecting Death Row.

How must we imagine this transmission? Can you tell about your own experiences?

Let us get an understanding of the word "transmission". It means to send across, from one person, thing or place to another. Saint John in the Bible makes that point when he tells his disciples that Jesus will baptize with the Holy Spirit. In some Bible translations, they use the word "fire". The transmission is a spiritual process of initiation. That is the best way for you to imagine it or you can have that direct experience by taking an Intensive, a program offered in Siddha Yoga. Through the Master's divine will, there is an energy transmission into your own mind, body and soul that renews and transforms your experience of yourself and others. After this spiritual transmission, your spiritual journey begins in earnest.

About my own experience, I will share one with you. One time I was chanting in my cell for about two hours. After I finished chanting, I turned the light off and went to sleep. About 30 minutes later, I was awakened by water coming down from my ceiling. The water was blue and sprinkling. I don't have a hole or leak in my ceiling. I felt the water hitting my face and body, but I was not wet. I got up and turned on the light and everything was back to normal. There are many experiences like this in Siddha Yoga. But it's not just an experience to talk about and to tell others about. It was a profound gift from the Guru of cleansing and purification.

Speaking about receiving spiritual power from the Guru, what is the importance of our own efforts to develop spiritual awakening?

You have to be sincere, humble and most of all have a desire to want to learn about who you are and your purpose in this life. There is a proverb that says, "When the disciple is ready, the Master will appear". Meditating and chanting the Guru's mantra is a sure way to develop spiritual awareness of one's own divine nature and the divine nature of everything around you.

A lot of people, when they hear the word "meditation" think about a strange and severe discipline. Can you tell more about your way of meditating? Do you have some special procedures or exercises to prepare for meditation that you can share with us?

Meditation for me comes naturally. It is spontaneous. There are no rituals or ceremonies I have to do. All I have to do is sit down, close my eyes and meditate on my Self with the awareness, "I am Shiva". This is called Siddha meditation. If you sit with the intention to meditate, then meditation will happen. Some people become frustrated because they are not able to achieve a quiet mind right away.

Don't let that frustrate you. Baba Muktananda said, "Whenever you sit for meditation, whatever comes up is meditation".

Begin by taking a comfortable upright posture, on the floor or in a chair. Take several nice deep breaths in and out and begin to look within for discomfort in the mind and body. If you find a place of mental or physical discomfort, just breath into that place until you feel that you have "let go" of the discomfort. In this way, the mind and body will start to release its tension and meditation will spontaneously arise. In Siddha Yoga meditation, we take the aid of the mantra, "Om Namah Shivaya" and repeat it silently once as we breathe in and again as we breathe out. This great mantra literally means," I bow to God who dwells within my own being." When you offer this beautiful phrase to the mind over and over again, the mind finally lets go of all the illusory thoughts and settles into itself. Don't fight what comes up; just go with it and observe your thoughts like waves on an ocean, rising and subsiding. Keep offering the mantra to the mind, and you will find peace. Just start with a few minutes every day, preferably in the morning and continue to add time to your meditation as you are able to. I like to meditate for one hour per day, but I have built up this practice over the years.

Often people argue that their religion or spiritual practice is the only way to connect with God. What are your thoughts on that?

If this is what they believe, then for them, they are absolutely right! However, this type of thinking is dangerous and destructive if they believe that their religion is the only way for everyone everywhere to connect with God! The Middle East is a prime example of religious thoughts and ideas clashing together. Millions of people have lost their lives in so-called holy wars. There are true saints of every religion and there are many ways to connect with God. The fastest way is turning within. The Bible says, "He who dwells in the secret place of the Most High shall abide under the shadow of the Almighty". The secret place is the heart. If you are looking to connect with God, you can find him in your heart.

You also meditate on the chakras. What is their importance?

The importance of the chakras is to raise the Kundalini life force from the Muladhara Chakra at the base of the spine to the Sahasrara chakra in the crown of the head. It is in these chakras, when meditated on, a person can experience various qualities of love, bliss, joy and different planes of consciousness are also experienced. In Siddha Yoga meditation, the kundalini energy is awakened and so it travels spontaneously up and down the seven chakras constantly purifying them. That's what's so great about having a Siddha Guru - you don't have to make anything happen because it happens spontaneously according to exactly what you need at the time.

How do you meditate on the chakras? Can you tell me about your experiences?

There are several ways to meditate on the chakras. Sitting down, laying down or standing up. I prefer meditating on the chakras sitting down. First, I visualize each chakra along the spine. You have to have a general idea on where the chakras are located on the spine. Note: The chakras are in the astral body. When I visualize the chakras I begin to chant the seed letters in each chakra starting with the Muladhara up to the Ajna. *Lam, van, ram yam, ham and Om*. In this way, the chakras are activated one by one.

I will tell you one of my experiences. One day while I was meditating on the chakras, I found myself standing on the top of a giant lotus flower and all of a sudden, it began to move very fast rising up like an elevator. It stopped at the Ajna Chakra where I was able to look out into the Universe as if I was looking through a telescope. Everything was blue and the colors were very bright. After a minute of observing the Universe, the telescope (third eye) closed and the giant lotus flower began to slowly descend back to the Muladhara Chakra.

A lot of people who are interested in practicing yoga ask if yoga has something to do with religion. Can you practice yoga being a Christian, Muslim, etc.? And what is the relation between yoga and religion?

Yoga is the foundation of all religions. There are many Muslims, Christians and Jews who practice Yoga. The word religious is from the Latin *religare* which means to bind. People are trying to bind themselves back to God and so they practice yoga knowing that it will give them the experience of God. Someone who loves Jesus and meditate on him will have a divine experience of Jesus; someone who meditates on Allah will experience the divinity in their own hearts of Allah. Meditation is for everyone!

Pete, you say there are many ways to connect with God and you recommend the

way by turning within. How can the yogic experience be helpful with that?

The experience is helpful because it destroys all doubt about what man thought he knew about God. There are many ways to connect with God, but in the end you will have to turn within to experience your own personal divine connection. You can listen to the preachers and read the words of the scriptures, but in the end your own direct experience of God will be your true lifeline. Otherwise, how will you ever know for sure? And the practices of yoga are meant to lead you to direct experiences of whoever you believe God to be.

Some people, especially in the western world, have placed God in heaven. That is a comfortable situation, because they feel free to act as they choose. What is your point of view on that?

The western world is disconnected from God. A lot of people believe they have to die to go to meet God in heaven, not understanding that the very God they speak of dwells within the heart. There are people who sincerely preach about God, but they believe God is other than themselves. This thinking is what keeps man disconnected from God. When man understands that God dwells in the heart, he will not be worried about dying and going to heaven. When a person has a deep conviction that God dwells within their own heart, they cannot help but experience God in everyone else's heart as well. "As within, so without."

"Oneness" is an important word in Siddha Yoga. And yet, people see many different things and persons and still don't see God in it. How can you explain that?

There is only one word that can explain that and that word is *maya. Maya* is the force that projects multiplicity and separation from God. "That guy is richer than me, I'll never get him to like me, I don't my job." These are all phrases reflecting a belief in separation from God and one another. In the Guru Gita verse 10, it says, "Maya - the creator of the world, the veiled knowledge born of ignorance - resides in the body. He whose light (true knowledge) arises is known by the word, 'Guru'." Knowledge means to know, to be aware. It also means light. As long as the veil exists that covers the light, man will never see or experience oneness. "Oneness" is knowing with complete conviction that God dwells within you and within everyone you meet. If God is within all, then all are one and there is no separation. As hard as it may be to understand, you come to understand that the plight of Man is the same from person to person. We are not separate and this knowledge brings great peace. You cannot be better than someone else and they cannot be better than you because you are both one and the same. And the nature of who you are is Love. That's the good news!

In some religions, the community and the experience of unity is a way to come closer to God. Does the community also play an important role in Siddha Yoga?

Community is very important in Siddha Yoga. Those who pray/meditate together, stay together. Jesus said, "A house divided against itself will not stand". If the community is divided amongst itself, then it's impossible to experience the love and unity that comes from working and being together. That's why in Siddha Yoga, we have a weekly program called *satsang* where everybody comes together to chant, meditate and to read the scriptures. We offer *seva*, selfless service, together and through our close relationships, we draw closer to God.

Chapter 7 The Precepts of the Gurus

"To understand a proverb and an enigma, pay attention to the words of the wise and their riddles."

- King Solomon

The *Precepts of the Gurus* were written over nine hundred years ago by a Tibetan yogi named Dvapo-Lharje, also known as the great Guru Gampopa. There are twenty eight categories of the *Yogic Precepts*. Each category has ten or more precepts that totals over two hundred. Out of the twenty-eight categories, I have chosen fifteen precepts for individuals that are incarcerated, along with scriptures, and a brief commentary. These precepts are to be meditated on and incorporated within our daily lives.

1. "The holy Guru being the guide on the Path, it would be a cause of regret to be separated from him before attaining enlightenment." In the Bible, Mathew 14:28-31, "And Peter answered Him and said, "Lord, if it is you, command me to come to you on the water."So he said, Come". And when Peter had come down out of the boat, he walked on the water to

go to Jesus. But, when he saw that the wind was boisterous, he was afraid; and beginning to sink, he cried out, saying, "Lord, save me!". And immediately Jesus stretched out his hand and caught him, and said to him, "O you of little faith, why did you doubt?"

Jesus is the holy Guru, the spiritual Master, the guide, the way, the truth and the life. The Path or way is the Yogic Science. Peter separated himself from Jesus when he took his eyes (his concentration) off of Jesus, and then, as he began to have doubts, he began to sink. Thus, it would be a cause of regret if you separate your mind and heart from the Guru.

2. "Inasmuch as all beings are our kindly parents, it would be a cause of regret to have aversion for and thus disown or abandon any of them." In the Bible, Mar 3:35, "For whosoever does the will of God, is my brother and my sister and mother".

Want for your brother what you want for yourself. Do unto others as you would have them do unto you. What man does for man, he does for God, and when man disrespects man, he disrespects God. Your brother is one who does the will of God. In order to do the will of God, you have to be in tune with God, and this is possible through meditation. This precept talks about all beings being our parents. Our parents are our first teachers, so therefore all being are our teachers. We can learn from everyone and every situation. Who can teach you more about the hazards of drinking, someone who abstains or someone who has lost everything to drink? Some of the most difficult people in our lives are our greatest teachers.

3. "Unceasing watchfulness and mental alertness, graced with humility are required to keep the body, speech and mind unsullied by evil." In the Bible, Mathew 26:41, "Watch and pray lest you enter into temptation. The Spirit indeed is willing, but the flesh is weak".

Concentrate, meditate, and stay God-conscious, thus setting up positive vibrations within and around your entire being. This precept is telling you to protect your positive state of mind. Remain vigilant to people and events that would lead you away from your own goodness.

4. "See friends who have beliefs and habits like thine own and in whom thou canst place thy trust." In the Bible, Psalm 133:1, "Behold, how good and how pleasant it is for brethren to dwell together in unity."

Those who meditate and pray together, stay together. It is good to seek the company of people that are firm on the spiritual path. This helps you to maintain your own personal focus.

5. "Study the teachings of the great sages of all sects impartially." In the Bible, 2 Timothy 3:16-17, "All scripture is given by inspiration of God, and is profitable for doctrine, for reproof, for correction. For instruction in righteousness, that the man of God may be complete, thoroughly equipped for every good work".

 Study the great words of the sages of all religions and sects. From this you will know that the basis of the world's religions is love and peace. Man has twisted these great works for his own purposes, but the original words of the saints are pure and consistent from religion to religion. Seek knowledge from the cradle to the grave. God is present in all religions. Each religion is a road that leads to God.

6. "Adopt such devotional practices as will be conducive to thy spiritual development." In the Qur'an, Surah 76:25-26, "And celebrate the name of your Lord morning and evening, and part of the night prostrate yourself to him and glorify him a long night through".

To develop oneself spiritually, continue to meditate, pray and read the scriptural texts. Chant the name of the Lord. Create your own program of spiritual practices and discipline, one that personally works for you. Is it getting up a little earlier to meditate or staying up a little later to read the scriptures?

7. "This human life in the Kali-yuga (age of Darkness) being so brief and uncertain, it would be a cause of regret to spend it in worldly aims and pursuits." In the Qur'an, Surah 56:20, "Know that the life of this world is but play and amusement, pomp and mutual boasting and multiplying (in rivalry) among yourselves riches and children".

As long as we continue to attach ourselves to things that are impermanent, we will never have peace. Each day of this life is a precious opportunity to become closer to God. Know that each moment presents a new opportunity to "choose God". Take awareness of God everywhere, into your daily activities and into your sleep and into what you eat. Your life will be transformed.

8. "One must know that attachment to worldly things maketh material prosperity inimical to spiritual progress." In the Bible, Luke 18:24-25, "How hard it is for those who have riches to enter the kingdom of God. For it is easier for a camel to go through the eye of a needle than for a rich man to enter the kingdom of God."

In order to make progress on the spiritual path, you have to let go of the things that are holding you back.

9. "Seek a delightful solitude endowed with psychic influences as a hermitage". In the Bible, Psalms 23:6, I will dwell in the house of the Lord forever".

The ashram, the church, the synagogue, mosque or a quiet serene corner in your own home, are good places to seek solitude.

10. "Avoid friends and followers who are detrimental to thy peace of mind and spiritual growth." In the Qur'an, Surah 28:55, "And when they hear vain talk, they turn away from there and say: To us our deeds, and to you yours, peace be to you, we seek not the ignorant."

Separate yourself from people that are unstable and trouble makers. These people are restless, and mean you no good. They will interfere with your peace of mind.

11. "Novices should persevere in listening to, and meditating upon, religious teachings." In the Bible, Psalm 119:15, "I will meditate on your precepts, and contemplate your ways."

Listen with your inner ear, and meditate on the word of God within the scriptures.

12. "For one of little intellect, the best thing is to have faith in the law of cause and effect." In the Bible, Galatians 6:7, "Do not be deceived, God is not mocked, for whatever a man sows, that he will also reap".

The world we live in operates under the law of cause an effect, and by understanding the law, our actions become pure when dealing with others.

13. "For one of ordinary intellect, the best thing is to recognize both within and without oneself, the workings of the law of opposites." In the Bible, Mathew 18:18, "Assuredly, I say to you, whatever you bind on earth will be bound in heaven, and whatever you loose on earth will be loosed in heaven".

Opposites are identical in nature, but different in degree. As above, so below, as below, so above.

14. "Those who outwardly profess, but do not practice religion may be mistaken for true devotees." In the Bible, James 1:22, "But be doers of the Word, and not heavens only, deceiving yourself".

Practice what you preach. Do not profess a religion and try to teach others that which you yourself are not practicing.

15. "Meditation without sufficient preparation through having heard and pondered the doctrine is apt to lead to the error of losing oneself in the darkness of unconsciousness." In the Bible, Mark 14:38, "Watch and pry lest you enter into temptation. The Spirit indeed is willing but the flesh is weak".

If you sit for mediation without the proper preparations then the mind becomes tempted by its own thoughts. The best preparation before meditation is chanting the name of God.

Questions for personal study:

1. What are the precepts of the Gurus?
2. How do we incorporate the precepts in our life?
3. Is it possible to live by the precepts?
4. Which one of the precepts do you think is hard to follow and why?
5. Choose one precept that you can relate to. Try to incorporate this precept into your daily life. Make a plan of action - one that you can easily follow.

Chapter 8 The Origin of Confusion

"This devine Maya of mine is difficult to overcome. Those who take refuge I me alone can overcome it"

- The Bhagavad Gita

The fall of man is one of many stories that shows how Man, the individual soul, separated himself from God. In reality, the soul can never separate from God. The Scriptures say that the individual soul is not a separate entity from God. Swami Prabhupada says, "The difference between God and the Soul is that God is a very great Soul, and the living entity is a very small soul; but qualitatively, they are equal. God is all-pervading, and the living entity is localized. But the nature and quality are the same."

Now, because of *maya* or illusion, man has forgotten his oneness with God. *Maya* is the force that conceals or veils our true divinity. It makes us believe God is other than our Self. A good example of man's forgetfulness is when one of Jesus' disciples asked him, "Lord, show us the Father and it is sufficient for us." Jesus replied, "He who has seen me has seen the Father." So, how can you say, "Show us the Father"? In the movie *The Wizard of Oz,*

Dorothy and her friends were all under the spell of *maya*. They did not know who the wizard was, until they looked behind the curtain and saw that the Wizard was just like them. The *yellow brick road* is the spiritual path that everyone must travel in order to reconnect with God. It is the only road; there are no short cuts. We all go through the forest to get to the light.

In the divine words of Swami Muktananda, "God dwells within you as you." Some people still believe in the *man upstairs*. I used to share the same belief, until I received *shaktipat initiation*. When I received *shaktipat*, I came into the realization that God dwells with me and not upstairs. However, all the scriptures tell us that God dwells within us. In the Bible it says, "And what agreement has the temple of God with idols? For you are the temple of the living God. As God has said: "I will dwell in them and walk among them. I will be their God, and they shall be my people."

The first house of worship is Man. Turn within and meditate, and rise above the confusion. You will see that God is real, and not a mystery.

How do we go behind the curtain of *maya* and see God face to face? By meditation and contemplation. The Bible says: "Be still, and know that I am God."

Saint Teresa of Avila said, "You need not go to heaven to see God; nor need you speak loudly, as if God were far away, nor need you cry for wings like a dove to fly to him. Only be in silence, and you will come upon God within yourself."

How does one find silence on Death Row? Or in a busy household? By going within and practicing meditation, you will find a profound silence that defies all the noises that surround us each day. And that silence will be with you when you come out of mediation and will accompany you as you go through your day. There is confusion all around you, but there is peace within yourself that you can access anytime.

Questions for personal study:

1. What is the origin of confusion?
2. Is the soul separated from God?
3. What is Maya and how do we overcome it?
4. The first house of worship is?

Chapter 9 Spiritual Warfare and Yoga

"For the flesh lusts against the Spirit, and the Spirit against the flesh and these are contrary to one another, so that you do not do the things that you wish."

- St. Paul

Throughout the history of mankind, there have been many wars fought for various reasons. Some wars are sincerely fought in the name of freedom, justice and equality while others are fought in the name of God, greed and oil. It is said everything is politics. To name a few of these wars, we have the Civil War, the Spanish American War, World War I and II, the Korean War, the Vietnam War, the Iraqi War, the Afghan War and the war on Terrorism. In all of these wars, hundreds of thousands of people, even millions have lost their lives, and families were destroyed. A trail of tears, suffering, death, destruction and bloodshed have occurred, all in the name of war.

This is the war that we read about and see on television. However there is another war taking place within that Man does not want to acknowledge. It is this war that man must win if he truly wants peace on earth. This war is called "spiritual warfare" by the Christians and the " internal holy war or *Jihad*" by the Muslims. The traditional weapons used on the physical battlefield, missiles, bombs, rockets and hand grenades, will not help man win the war on the spiritual battlefield.

Spiritual warfare is a spiritual battle that begins and ends within Man. When the individual soul makes a conscious choice to turn his life around and reconnect with God, war breaks out in the heavens between the higher Self and the lower Self. The reason for war is if the ego of Man allows the soul to reconnect with God-consciousness, then the ego will no longer exist.

The ego is strong and alive, as long as the soul is spiritually weak, and unconscious of his higher Self. The ego is in a fight to the death with the higher consciousness. Only one can be victorious.

This war is psychological and is taking place within the mind. We should also understand that the mind is the most powerful thing in the Universe, and that the wars, confusion and conflicts that we see on Earth are only a reflection and manifestation of what is taking place in the mind. You are not fighting with Satan or the devil. You are fighting against the ego. Satan and the devil are masks that the ego wears to fool you. So when the ego attacks you or persuades you to do something against your will, people blame the devil.

The ego is public enemy number one and his stronghold is in the lower Self. What Paul says is true - the lust or desire of the flesh is to keep the soul trapped in the lower Self, and the lust or desire of the spirit is to free the soul, so that it can merge back into the higher Self. These two are contrary to one another and the battle within becomes a tug of war over the Soul.

In this struggle, the entire spine becomes a battlefield, especially in the three lower chakras where the negative pull and the temptations are strongest. The Bhagavad Gita, Ch. 16:21, describes the lower Self as the threefold Gate of Hell. "Lust, anger and greed - these constitute the threefold gates of Hell leading to the destruction of the soul's welfare. These three, therefore, man should abandon."

In the book of James in the Bible, Ch. 1:12, it says "Blessed is the man who endures temptation, for when he has been approved, he will receive the crown of life which the Lord has promised to those who love Him."

Now the ego, under the mask of Satan tells Allah (God) what he planned to do to Man. In the Quran Sura7:16-17, he said he would lie in wait for Man on the straightway, or spiritual path. In verse 17, he describes his battle plan. He says, ""Then will I assault them from front and from behind them, from their right and their left and you will not find, in most of them gratitude (for your mercies)."

What are some of the weapons that the ego uses against the Soul? First, we must understand that the ego or Satan have no power over us. He can only tempt us or make suggestions, but it's up to us to accept or reject him.

The weapon of choice for the ego in his assault on Man is negative thoughts. Jealousy, hatred, worry, gossip, backbiting, doubt, fear, lying, sexual immorality, racism, selfishness, envy, and fault-finding. Keep in mind that this war is taking place within the mind. When the ego bombards the mind with its negative thoughts, Man becomes double-minded, and unstable in his thinking. Paul says, "So that you do not do the things that you wish."

The mind becomes split within itself allowing the pendulum to swing back and forth between thoughts of good and bad, love and hate, right and wrong. Thus the mind becomes stressed-out, restless and agitated or aggravated, as they say in prison. This state of mind effects the senses and nervous system, causing an imbalance, and "dis-ease" in the body. This sickness is seen in the world in the form of war, disease and stress.

In this spiritual battle against the ego, there are many weapons man can use. However, the weapon of choice is yoga. In the Yoga Sutras of Patanjali 1:2, it says, "Yoga is the restraint of fluctuations in the Mind". This definition of yoga is related to Psalms 46:10, which says, "Be Still, and know that I am God". To restrain is the same as to be still, meaning to cease or stop all activity. The individual on the spiritual battlefield must be able to control or neutralize the incoming flow of negative thoughts from the ego. These thoughts are the fluctuations or waves in the mind. When the thoughts are successfully restrained, the mind becomes still and God reveals himself to Man. This is the re-connection or yoga that the ego is trying to prevent man from having.

If Man goes to battle with the mind, the mind will always win. This is not a violent battle. It's a battle that takes place every moment, in the moment of choice. This is a battle that is won step-by-step, day by day. In each moment you offer the mind the highest thought, the highest attitude and the highest service. You do this repeatedly asking yourself how can you serve God in this moment. Over time, the ego softens and you come to know that this is a battle that you will win.

Questions for personal study:

1. How does the ego assault man? Where does the assault take place?
2. Where does spiritual warfare take place?
3. What happens when an individual begins to turn his life around?
4. What is the weapon of choice we can use against the ego?
5. In the Bhagavad Gita, what are the characteristics of the lower Self?
6. Do you believe you can win the battle over the ego? Why?

Chapter 10 Shaktipat Diksha

"He who, by his gracious look, touch or word
gives to the disciple an experience of his
identity with the Absolute, is indeed the Guru."
- *The Yoga Vasishtha*

Since the beginnings of time, Man has
created ceremonies and rituals, as a way of
initiating individuals into various schools,
clubs, lodges, and fraternities. Also, on the
spiritual path, you have religious ceremonies
and rituals that evolve around baptism, the
Eucharist, circumcision and sometimes walking
over hot coals, depending on the culture and
people. In all the scriptures known to Man, you
have some form of initiation that takes place
between the Guru and disciple. For example, in
the Koran you have Moses seeing initiation
from Melchizedek, the Priest of the Most High
God. Moses said, "May I follow you on the
conditions that you teach me something of the
higher truth which you have been taught?"

However, the highest form of initiation is *shaktipat diksha*. Swami Muktananda says, "Indeed, the process of *shaktipat diksha* is highly mysterious, secret and amazing."

I would like to point out two places in the Bible that show the Guru and disciples relationship and how the Guru gives Shaktipat Diksha to his disciple.

In the Bible, 2 Kings 2:9-13, you have the story of Elijah and Elisha. As you read, you will see Elisha receiving Shaktipat Diksha from Elijah.

Verse 9 - Elijah said unto Elisha, "Ask what I shall do for thee, before I be taken away from thee." And Elisha said, "I pray thee, let a <u>double</u> portion of thy Spirit (Shakti) be upon me."

Verse 10 - And He said, "Thou hast asked a hard thing. Nevertheless, if thou see me when I am taken from thee, it shall be so unto thee, but if not, it shall not be so."

Verse 11 - And it came to pass, as they still went on, and talked, that behold, there appeared a chariot of fire, and horses of fire and parted them both asunder, and Elijah went up by a whirlwind into heaven.

Verse 12 - And Elisha saw it, and he cried, "My Father, my Father, the Chariot of Israel and the horsemen thereof. And he saw him no more. And he took hold of his own clothes and rent them in two pieces.

Verse 13- He took up also the mantle of Elijah that fell from him and went back and stood by the bank of Jordan.

In Verse 15, the sons of the prophets said, "The spirit (*shakti*) of Elijah doth rest on Elisha." The sons of the prophets witnessed the initiation from afar. Did you see the initiation? If not, here is a definition for Diksha. It will help you understand what took place.

Diksha: Initiation, the spiritual awakening of the disciples by *shaktipat* through a look, word, thought or touch of the Guru.

Elisha received his double portion of spirit by looking at Elijah when he was taken away in a whirlwind. Elijah said, "if thou see me". This was the first portion of the spirit. The second portion was Elisha picking up the mantle of Elijah. Picking up the mantle is the same as touching Elijah, because the mantle is permeated with Elijah's spirit.

You also have in the Bible Jesus giving *shaktipat diksha* to his disciples, found in John 20: 21-22.

Verse 21 - So Jesus said to them again, "Peace to you! As the Father has sent me, I also send you."

Verse 22 - And when He had said this, He breathed on them and said to them, "Receive the Holy Spirit."

The breath and Holy Spirit are the same. It is through the breath of Jesus (the *prana*) that his disciples received *shaktipat*. What is *shaktipat*? *Shaktipat* is the "descent of grace" of the Master. It is the transmission of spiritual power or *shakti* from the Guru to the disciple, the spiritual awakening by grace. This is accomplished by the will of the Guru, the Master.

There is a dormant spiritual center that is present at the base of the spine in every human being. This spiritual center has been sleeping for ages and ages. And it coincides with the root *chakra* that we talked about earlier. When the Master bestows *shaktipat*, his or her spiritual energy enters the devotee and that dormant energy center at the base of the spine is awakened. Once awakened, a devotee's spiritual journey begins in earnest. The powerful energy that has been awakened begins it long and steady climb to the *sahasrara*, the crown *chakra* located at the top of the head. As it climbs, a process of purification begins and everything that happens in a devotee's life after the gift of *shaktipat* takes on a new and divine meaning.

The old cycle of life and death is now broken and Man begins his journey to self-realization and the knowledge that he and God are one and the same. Moments of bliss and love occur and a peace slowly but surely comes into a life where there was only strife and worry before. Over the lifetime of one who has received *shaktipat,* the pull of the material world begins to fall away and the true virtues of life including love, wisdom and compassion begin to take its place. This is a process which occurs naturally and spontaneously in the life of a devotee who has chosen to follow a true Master, one who has completed their own journey and can lead and show others the way.

Someone who has received *shaktipat* does not become weak and unable to defend themselves because of their love for the Holy Spirit. On the contrary, wisdom takes the place of anger and they are able to act with a new strength and conviction. The virtues rise up to meet such a person and their life becomes, over time, filled with integrity and purpose. They are able to set an example of a life well-lived. Through their very presence, they can touch the hearts of others and are able to offer peace and contentment as a result of the fruits of their own spiritual practices - the practices of meditation and chanting. Wherever they go, they are accompanied by the grace-bestowing power of the *shakti,* whose only purpose is to uplift and serve mankind.

Jesus gave the word, "Receive the Holy Spirit" and his spirit was transmitted into his disciples. The *prana* or breath is the vital life-sustaining force of both the individual body and the entire universe. This is the same prana God breathed into the nostrils of Adam and Adam became a living soul. You can receive *shaktipat diksha* too, by seeking the lotus feet of Gurumayi, the living Master of the Siddha Yoga lineage.

Questions for personal study:
1. What is shaktipat diksha?
2. What did Elisha pray for?
3. How was Elisha initiated and what happened after?
4. How did Jesus initiate his disciples?
5. After Jesus initiated his disciples, what did he say to them?

Chapter 11 My Experience of Shaktipat Diksha Initiation

"Most assuredly, I say to you, unless one is born again, he cannot see the Kingdom of God."

- Jesus

Regardless of time and place, when the student is ready the Guru will come. I will never forget. It was in the year 2005 that I received *shaktipat* initiation from Gurumayi. Gurumayi Chidvilasananda, of the Siddha Yoga lineage of Masters, is my Guru. She is a powerful Siddha that gives Shaktipat to thousands of people around the world. Because I had a strong desire to know God, the Guru came and initiated me on the path of Siddha Yoga.

I have decided to write about my initiation, so that I could share my story and experience with others. My story in essence is a universal teaching. It's nothing new. My initiation reflects the truth of the scriptures in which Jesus says, "unless one is born again, he cannot see the Kingdom of God".

Over two thousand years ago, Jesus told a man by the name of Nicodemus that he had to be born again in order to see the Kingdom of God. Like many people today, Nicodemus was confused. He did not understand what Jesus said about being born again. Nicodemus asked Jesus, How can a man be born when he is old? Can he enter a second time into his mother's womb and be born?" Jesus answered, "Most assuredly, I say to you, unless one is born of water and the spirit, he cannot enter the kingdom of God".

What does it really mean to be born again? Have you ever been born again? If so, did you see the Kingdom of God? If you have never seen the Kingdom of God, then there is a strong possibility that you were never born again. I am not judging anyone. I am only telling you what Jesus said according to the yogic science which he taught.

To see the Kingdom of God is to have a direct experience, a mystical experience of the kingdom within yourself. In the Bible, Luke 17:21 Jesus said, "Nor will they say, see, hear or see there! For indeed the Kingdom of God is within you".

Swami Vivekananda says, "After long searches here and there, in temples and churches, in earths and in heavens, at last you come back completing the circle from where you started, to your own soul and find that He, for whom you have been weeping and praying in churches and temples, on whom you were looking as the mystery of all mysteries shrouded in the clouds, is nearest of the near, is your own Self, the reality of your life, body and soul".

As I stated before, it was in the year 2005 that I received Shaktipat from Gurumayi. By receiving Shaktipat, I was allowed to see the kingdom of God or should I say blessed to see the kingdom of God within myself. I want you to understand that *Shaktipat* initiation, imparted to me by the will of my Guru, was the key to my spiritual experiences on that day and on every day since. It is the same Holy Spirit or fire that John the Baptist said Jesus would use.

I was in my cell alone as always. Here on Death Row, every man is always alone. I prepared myself as usual for a period of meditation. I washed my hands, face and feet. The time was around 10 p.m. I always use mala beads which are an aid in the repetition of the mantra; in Catholicism they are called rosary beads. I set up my photo of Gurumayi and I sat down cross-legged on my bed. I stared at the picture of Gurumayi and, holding my mala beads, began chanting the mantra of the Siddha lineage, *Om Namah Shivaya*, which literally means "I bow to God, who dwells within my own being." Gurumayi has told us to repeat it silently in time with the breath, once as you breathe in and again as you breathe out. I sat like this for an hour or more, repeating the mantra, breathing in and out.

After sitting and chanting like this for a while, something strange began to happen. My lower back became very hot and the heat started to spread throughout my back. I continued to chant. A vision came to me and I could clearly see the *kundalini* energy rising from the base of my spine. My physical eyes were open, but I was seeing inside of my body with my divine eyes. The color of this energy was reddish-orange. I continued to repeat the mantra *Om Namah Shivaya* as this beautiful reddish-orange energy rose up my spine. I could hear the sound of each *chakra* as the energy passed through and with that sound, they each opened one by one.

The energy reached the top of my spine and I began to cry tears of joy like I had never experienced before. Tears flowed silently from my eyes and I felt immense waves of a love I had never felt before. It wasn't a love associated with desire; it was a pure, free-flowing love that existed within me. I continued to repeat *Om Namah Shivaya*. The energy was now in the top of my head, the *sahasrara,* and all at once there was a loud sound and a flash of blinding, white light.

I began to experience very strong movements, called *kriyas.* I felt my body being lifted up and down on my bunk. I sought to control myself, but my body was moving independently of my will and I could do nothing to stop it. I finally fell to the floor and continued to shake.

These movements lasted about three minutes and finally they stopped. I got back on my bunk and began to stare at Gurumayi's picture once more and again, the *kriyas* started within. This time they lasted for about a minute. I had fallen off of my bunk again. I got back on my bunk and this time when I looked at the Guru's picture, my legs locked into the lotus position, with both feet on my thighs.

Swami Muktananda writes, "When the *kundalini shakti* is awakened, many different movements or *kriyas*, take place in the gross body. These *kriyas* are not meaningless, they destroy sickness and purify the nadis."

From this great awakening that took place inside of me, I knew that I had experienced the kingdom of God. I saw the light and became one with the light. That light exists and it is pure consciousness. I understand now when the sages and saints say that God is brighter than a thousand suns because I have experienced this light. I have experienced the kingdom of God within my own being. Within this very body, that sits from day to day in a cell alone on Texas Death row, I have experienced overwhelming love, peace and joy.

My experience of shaktipat diksha was very strong and each person's experience is different. Sometimes *shaktipat* is very mild and other times it's very powerful, like my experience. Each person receives exactly what they need when they receive this great initiation.

Questions for personal study:

1. Spiritually speaking, have you ever been initiated?
2. What does it mean to be born again?
3. What is the meaning of Jesus' words to Nicodemus?
4. What is your interpretation of the words *Om Namah Shivaya*?
5. Where is the kingdom of God?

Chapter 12 The Chakras

"Who is the Lord of the Seven Heavens (Chakras) and the Lord of the Throne of Glory Supreme?"

-The Qur'an

I am writing about the *chakras* because I would like everyone to become aware of them during their daily meditation or, if possible, take the Intensive program which Siddha Yoga offers once a year. When I received *shaktipat* from my Guru, all of my *chakras* began to open one by one. The experience reminds me of a question in the book of Revelation. "Who is worthy to open the scroll and to loose its seals". The answer to that question is the *sadguru* or true Guru. The scriptures state that the Guru is the grace bestowing power of God. So it is the grace of God through the Guru that sets you on the path of liberation.

Shri Ramakrishna gives a in depth description of the *chakras*. "In the scripture, mention is made of the *Seven Centers of Consciousness*. When the mind is attached to worldliness, consciousness dwells in the three lower centers, the plexus sacracoccygeal, sacral and solar. During this time, there are no pure thoughts or high ideals that dwell there. It remains immersed in lust and greed. The fourth center of consciousness is the region of the heart. Spiritual awakening occurs when the mind rises to this center. At this stage, Man has a spiritual vision of the divine light and is struck with wonder at its beauty and glory. His mind then no longer runs after worldly pleasures. The region of the throat is the fifth center of consciousness. When the mind rises to this center, Man becomes free from nescience and ignorance. He then talks only on subjects relating to God and grows impatient if any worldly topic is discussed. He avoids hearing about worldly subjects. The sixth center is between the eyebrows. When the mind rises to this center, man becomes merged in Divine Consciousness. There is still left in him, however, the consciousness of being a separate being from God. Seeing the beatific vision of God, he becomes filled with joy and longs to come closer to him and be united with him. But he cannot, for there is still the ego which stands between them. One may compare God to the light in a lantern. You seem to feel its warmth; yet, though you wish to do so, you cannot touch it. because of the glass intervening. The center located in the top of the head is the seventh center. When one rises to this place, there is *samadhi.* That is the transcendental consciousness in which one realizes his oneness with God.

I will now give a definition and summary of the *chakras*:

1. *Muladhara Chakra* - the spiritual center at the base of the spine where Kundalini lies dormant and in a coiled form like a serpent.

Color: Yellow

Deity: Brahma

Bija mantra: lam

Element: earth

petals: 4

letters: 4

Shape of mandala: square

Function: smell

2. *Svadhistana Chakra* - the energy center within the sushumna in the sacral area.

Color: white

Deity: Vishnu

Bija Mantra: Vam

Element: Water

Petals: 6

Letters: 6

Shape of Mandala: Crescent moon

Function: taste

Activity: Svadisthana stands for feeling and sexuality. When it is open, feelings are flowing freely and are expressed without overreactions. When is it underactive, you tend to be stiff and unemotional and are not very open to people. When it is over-active, you tend to be emotional all the time.

3. *Manipura Chakra* - the spiritual center located in the navel region.

Color: red

Deity: Rudra

Bija Mantra: Ram

Element: Fire

Petals: 10

Letters: 10

Shape of Mandala: Triangle

Function: sight

Activity: Manipura stands for asserting yourself in a group. When it is open, you feel in control and have sufficient self esteem. When it is underactive, you tend to be passive and indecisive. When it is over-active, you tend to be overly dominant.

4. *Anahata Chakra* - the spiritual center located at the heart. The unstruck (anahata) sound heard in meditation originates in this center.

Color: smoky

Deity: Isha

Bija Mantra: Yam

Element: Air

Petals: 12

Letters: 12

Shape of Mandala: Hexagon

Function: touch

Activity: Anahata stands for love, kindness and affection. When it is open, you are compassionate and friendly. When it is underactive, you are cold and distant. When it is overactive, you tend to suffocate others with affection and attention and your expression of love can have selfish foundations.

5. *Vishuddha Chakra* - the energy center at the base of the throat.

Color: Blue

Deity: Shiva

Bija Mantra: ham

Element: ether

Petals: 16

Letters: 16

Shape of Mandala: round

Function: hearing

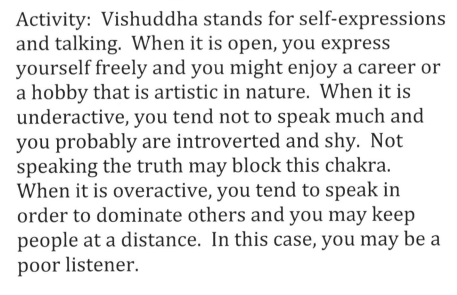

Activity: Vishuddha stands for self-expressions and talking. When it is open, you express yourself freely and you might enjoy a career or a hobby that is artistic in nature. When it is underactive, you tend not to speak much and you probably are introverted and shy. Not speaking the truth may block this chakra. When it is overactive, you tend to speak in order to dominate others and you may keep people at a distance. In this case, you may be a poor listener.

6. *Ajna Chakra* - the spiritual center located between the eyebrows. The awakened Kundalini passes through this chakra only by the command of the Guru.

Color: White or Bluish White

Deity: Shambhu

Bija Mantra: Om or Aum

Element: Mind

Petals: 2

Letters: 2

Shape of Mandala: Round

Activity: Ajna stands for insights and visualization. When it is open, you have good intuition. When it is underactive, you have trouble thinking for yourself and you may tend to rely too much on authority figures. You may be rigid in your thinking, relying on rules and beliefs too much. You may get confused easily. When it is overactive, you may live too much in a fantasy world.

7. *The Sahasrara*: the thousand-petaled lotus at the crown of the head. This is the highest spiritual center in a human being, where the union of Shiva and Shakti takes place.

Activity: When the individual soul reaches this spiritual center, he experiences supreme bliss and oneness with God. This is called samadhi. In this meditative state, a human being realizes that everything is supreme consciousness, pervaded by God.

The word "Sahasrara" means *one thousand,* because the center has a thousand petals. All of the fifty letters of the Sanskrit alphabet are in the *sahasrara* and repeated over twenty times. (20x50=1,000) Every prophet, sage and yogi who has reached the *sahasrara* in meditation has proclaimed that God is brighter than a thousand suns.

It is said that the great spiritual Masters live and dwell in the upper chakras. All of the world's illusions have burned away for them in the fires of meditation and they constantly dwell in the awareness of God, the awareness of the Self. When a Master is not engaged in daily activities, they close their eyes and look within, because what they see there is more beautiful than anything we can imagine. They are intoxicated by the beauty inside. This beauty is inside all of us and as the chakras become purified, one by one, we will begin to experience this inner beauty and know where the real treasure lies.

Questions for personal study:
1. How would you define the seven *chakras*?
2. Can you see the *chakras* with your physical eyes? If not, how do you see them?
3. Where are the *chakras* located?
4. What is the connection between Ezekiel's wheel and the *chakras*?
5. What is the name and nature of the seventh *chakra*?

Chapter 13 Ezekiel's Wheel

"For the spirit of the living creature was in the wheels."

- *Prophet Ezekiel*

I would like to shed some light on what Ezekiel saw concerning the wheels. For a long time man has been puzzled and confused about *Ezekiel's Wheel*. You have asked the clergy of pastors, bishops and rabbis about the wheel and you are still without a clear answer. If you were raised in the church or have studied the Bible, then you should be familiar with the story of Ezekiel's Wheel.

I would like to point out that the wheels in which Ezekiel is speaking about are the *chakras*. The word *chakra* in Sanskrit means wheel. These *chakras* are located in the astral body, not the physical body. You cannot see the *chakras* with the physical eyes. Only through concentration and deep meditation can you see them.

In the *Shiva Samhita* 4:26 it says:

The deities residing in the *chakras* (wheels) tremble (vibrate) when the *prana* (the vital life force) moves through the *sushumna* (spinal cord) and the great Goddess Kundalini (cosmic energy) is absorbed in Mount Kailas in the *sahasrara.* (the crown chakra located in the head).

In the first chapter of the book of Ezekiel, the wheels and creatures are explained in detail. Ezekiel said: "I was among the captives by the river of Chebar, that the heavens (chakras) were opened (pierced) and I saw visions of God."

The seven heavens, *chakras* and wheels are all the same. The scriptures speak of seven heavens. In the Bible 2 Corinthians 12:2, Paul knew a man that was taken to the third heaven. Paul says:

"I know a man in Christ (Christ consciousness or the ajna chakra) who fourteen years ago whether in the body, I do not know, or whether out of the body (astral body) I do not know, God knows - such a one was caught up (through meditation) to the third heaven (manipura chakra)."

The yogic science speaks of seven *chakras.* There are six important chakras: 1. Muladhara, 2 Svadhistana 3. Manipura 4. Anahata 5. Vishuddha and 6. Ajna. The Sahasrara chakra is the 7th chakra.

Now, the people that were captive with Ezekiel did not see the heavens open or visions of God. Remember, you cannot see the *chakras* with the physical eyes. Jesus said, "The kingdom of God does not come with observation". The kingdom of God and heaven are the same because the kingdom is in heaven. Jesus also said, "The kingdom of God is within you." This is important to understand. Everything that Ezekiel saw-the heavens, creatures, and visions of God took place within his own self. It was a spiritual event, not a physical one.

In the book of Revelation, John had the same experience as Ezekiel. Here are five verses to compare

1. Revelation 4:2 in comparison to Ezekiel 1:26

2. Revelation 4:3 in comparison to Ezekiel 1:28

3. Revelation 4:5 in comparison to Ezekiel 1:13

4. Revelation 4:7 in comparison to Ezekiel 1:10

5. Revelation 4:8 in comparison to Ezekiel 1:18

Revelation 4:2 "Immediately, I was in the spirit and behold, a throne was set in heaven and one sat on the throne."

Ezekiel 1:26 "And above the firmament that was over their heads was the likeness of a throne. As the appearance of a sapphire stone: and <u>upon the likeness of the throne was the likeness as the appearance of a man above it.</u>"

Revelation 4:3 "And he who sat there was like a Jasper and a Sardius Stone in appearance, and <u>there was a rainbow around the throne,</u> in appearance like an emerald."

Ezekiel 1:28 <u>"As the appearance of the bow that is in the cloud in the day of rain,</u> so was the appearance of the brightness round about."

Revelation 4:5 "And from the throne proceeded <u>lightening,</u> thundering, and voices. Seven <u>lamps of fire</u> were <u>burning</u> before the throne, which are the Seven Spirits of God."

Ezekiel 1:13 "As for the likeness of the living creatures, their appearance was like <u>burning coals of fire,</u> and like the appearance of <u>lamps:</u> it went up and down among the living creatures, and the fire was bright, and out of the fire went forth <u>lightening.</u>"

Revelation 4:7 "<u>The first living creature was like a lion, the second living creature like a calf, the third living creature had a face like a man, and the fourth living creature was like a flying eagle.</u>"

Ezekiel 1:10 "<u>As for the likeness of their faces, they four had the face of a man, and the face of</u>

a lion, on the right side; and they four had the face of an ox on the left side, they four also had the face of an eagle."

Revelation 4:8 "The four living creatures, each having six wings, were full of eyes around and within."

Ezekiel 1:18 "As for their rings, they were so high that they were dreadful, and their rings were full of eyes round about them four."

When we study the scriptures of the prophets, we find that they all had the same vision of Heaven and the *chakras*. In the Islamic literature, it states that Prophet Muhammad was transported from the sacred mosque (Kaba) to the mosque in Jerusalem. It is also said he was taken through the seven heavens/*chakras*, all the way to the sublime throne (the *sahasrara*). These mystic events are experienced in deep meditation. The Qur'an 17:1 states, "Glory to Allah who did take his servant for a journey by night from the sacred mosque to the farthest mosque, whose precincts we did bless in order that we might show him some of our signs, for he is the one who hears and sees all things."

Questions for personal study:

1. What is Ezekiel's wheel?
2. The wheels that Ezekiel saw; where were they located?
3. What is the name of the wheel Ezekiel saw?
4. How can we see Ezekiel's wheel?
5. Where did all of Ezekiel's visions take place?

Chapter 14 The Samskaras

"The impressions of past actions, stored deep in the mind, are the seeds of desire. They ripen into action in seen and unseen ways-if not in this life, then in a future one. As long as action leaves its seed in the mind, this seek will grow, generating more births, more lives, more actions."

-Sage Patanjali

"But each one (individual soul) is tempted when he is drawn away by his own desires and enticed. Then, when desire has conceived, it gives birth to sin and sin, when it is full grown, brings forth death."

-St. James

We are born into this world with a lot of karma. Your karma may be good or bad, depending on the *samskaras*. It is the *samskaras* that dictate whether your karma will be good or bad. The word *samskaras* literally means *impressions*. Every action, good or bad, leaves an impression on the soul. When our bad and good actions become balanced, the Master appears before us and we begin an upward ascent towards union with our own divine consciousness. This ascent begins when we receive *shaktipat diksha* initiation. Until then, we are souls that are trapped in the cycle of birth and death, living out our karma from lifetime to lifetime.

Inside each human being is the longing to know God. This longing is not just inside of people who we think of as "good". This desires lives within each and every one of us. It is this longing for union with God that eventually turns each human being around and gradually brings about the equalization of his good and bad actions. No one lives trapped within the cycle of birth and death forever. It is our soul's plan to one day unite with God and that plan propels us forward towards good actions.

When I was out on the streets in trouble with drugs and bad company, no one could see my longing to know God. Even I couldn't see it. But now I see it as my life's purpose, my only purpose. And the truth is, it was there inside of me all along.

Saint Paul is a good example on how the *samskaras* affect a person's life. Paul says in the Bible, 7:14-25.

Verse 14 - For we know that the law (universal law) is spiritual, but I am carnal (flesh/body) sold under sin (karma).

Verse 15 - For what I am doing, I do not understand (confused mental state). For what I will to do (seva, meditation, repetition of the name of God) that I do not practice, but what I hate (gossip, slander, self-righteousness) that I do.

Verse 16 - If, then, I do what I will not to do, I agree with the law (of cause and effect) that it is good.

Verse 17- But now, it is no longer I who do it, but sin (karma) that dwells (inside the subtle body) in me.

Verse 18 - For I know that in me (that is, in my subtle body) nothing good dwells, for to will is present within me (the spirit within Man is indeed willing to help) but how to perform what is good (meditation and prayer) I do not find (because of the strong identification and attachment to the body - the flesh is weak, therefore I am not able to will or perform what is good).

Verse 19 - For the good that I will to do (selfless service, helping others) I do not do, but the evil (hurting others) I will not to do, that I practice.

Verse 20 - Now if I do what I will not to do, it is no longer I who do it, but sin (seeds of desire, the impressions made on the conscious and subconscious mind by past thoughts and actions) that dwells in me.

Verse 21 - I find then a law that evil (impure thoughts and actions) is present with me, the one who wills to do good.

Verse 22 - For I delight (through meditation) in the law of God according to the inward (the Supreme Self) Man.

Verse 23 - But I see another law (the lower Self) in my members (the body) warring against the law of my mind (God consciousness) and bringing me (leading me away from God consciousness) into captivity (unconsciousness) to the law of sin which is in my members.

Verse 24 - O wretched (confused) Man that I am. Who will deliver me from this body of death? (the Guru!)

Verse 25 - I thank God - through Jesus Christ our Lord! So then with the mind (discrimination of the intellect) I myself serve (humbly obey) the law of God, but with the flesh the law of sin.

Now that we have an understanding of the *samskaras* and how they work in a human life, the next step is to purify (uproot the seeds of desire) the mind through meditation.

Swami Kripananda says, "The fire of meditation burns up the impurities of the mind, negative tendencies and old *samskara*s, or past impressions."

Gurumayi says, "When you meditate more and more, the fire of yoga is kindled inside, and this fire burns away negative karma. Negative karma is not just the guilt that we carry around; it is the hidden sadness that comes up and the hidden anger and pride. Only this inner fire can burn them away."

You can imagine that the karma among the Death Row inmates is very dark and dense. In some lives here, there have been very few good acts and many selfish ones. But one thing we have here on Death Row is the time to think.

Our thoughts can take us in many directions, but in the end there is nowhere to run and we must face the responsibility of our past actions. There is very little here to distract us and so we begin to look carefully at our own lives. By thinking about our past actions, we re-live events and feel the weight of our samskaras. But we also see that we did not start out this way. As children and young adults we had hope for the future, like everyone else. How did we end up here and how did you end up out there? This can only be answered by understanding our samskaras and our karma. I cannot say exactly what brought me here. Yes, there was a crime and a jury and a sentence of death by execution. But there is so much more to my story and my life that has brought me to this moment. And it's the same for you. As we go on the spiritual journey, the answers to these questions begin to be answered and we begin to experience peace within ourselves and we are able to look on others who made have caused us harm with love and compassion. This is the benefit of meditation. It burns up the old impressions and we are free to see and understand clearly what it means to have a human life.

Questions for personal study:

1. What are the *samskaras* and how do they affect people's lives?
2. Can you name a *samskara* that is active in your life?
3. Where are the *samskaras* located?
4. What is the best way to overcome the *samskaras*?
5. How are we tempted as human beings?

Chapter 15 Karma and Reincarnation

"Whatsoever a man soweth, that shall he also reap."

- *St. Paul*

"And to every soul will be paid in full (the fruit) of its deeds; and Allah knows best all that they do."

-Qur'an

There are many people in America who do not believe in the law of *karma*. When they hear the word "karma" or someone talking about karma, they immediately state that they don't believe in karma or there is no such thing. However, they believe whole heartedly in the law of gravity although gravity like oxygen is not a thing that can be seen.

Why is it so hard for people to believe in karma? This may sound strange but there are people who believe in karma unconsciously. My mother is one of those people. She doesn't believe in karma, but she will say things like, "what goes around comes around" and "you made your bed, so now lay in it". So you see, she really does believe in karma.

The word *karma* literally means "action. The law of karma is the law of cause and effect. The whole world runs under the law of karma. For every action, there is a reaction, be it physical, mental, or verbal. Man is the creator of his own heaven or hell. If you find yourself in heaven, that means your karma (your actions) were good here on earth. If you find yourself in hell that means your karma was bad here on earth.

The Qur'an says, "Whatever misfortune happens to you is because of the things your hands have done." Some people believe that their misfortune comes from God. Every time something goes wrong in their life they blame God. It is always, "Why God?, why God?". When something good happens they want to take credit for it. The Upanishads say:

"According as a man acts and walks in the path of life, so he becomes. He that does good becomes good, he that does evil becomes evil. By pure actions he becomes pure, by evil actions, he becomes evil."

The law of karma is simple. For every action, there is a reaction. Karma is the cosmic equalizer. That is why the scriptures say that

God is just God; a being that doesn't punish anyone. Man punishes himself through his words, acts and deeds. The Qur'an says:

"If anyone does a righteous deed, it ensures to the benefit of his own soul; if he does evil, it works against his own soul."

The law of karma should be taught at an early age at home and school. If people were raised with an understanding of karma, then they would be mindful of the things they say and do to each other. They would take responsibility for their own actions, instead of blaming others.

Reincarnation, like karma, is also rejected by the majority of people here in the West. This rejection is a sign of misinformation, falsehood, and half-truths taught by people who have no knowledge of the subject. These are the people, namely the Christian Right, who are always talking against the New Age religion. In reality, there is nothing new about it.

The belief in reincarnation is the belief that a soul will return to earth over and over again in order to experience and work out karma. The experiences of past lifetimes will determine the experiences in the lifetimes to come. A soul will take a different body each time, be born in a different location and have different experiences in order to learn the lessons that need to be learned so that he may advance on the spiritual path. Someone may experience the life of a drug addict over and over again until he is finally ready to move upward. Your wife in one life may be your cousin in another. The mysteries of reincarnation are vast and deep. Reincarnation is a science that has been around for thousands of years. It is a common belief in the East, and in all of the three major scriptures of the world: the holy Qur'an, the Bhagavad Gita, and the Christian Bible. All speak of reincarnation. The Qur'an says:

"And you were dead, and he brought you back to life. And he shall cause you to die, and shall bring you back to life, and in the end shall gather you unto himself."

In the Bhagavad Gita it says, "Certain is the death for the born, and certain is birth for the dead. When one is born, death follows, when one dies, rebirth follows."

The Bible says, "For all the prophets and the law prophesied until John. And if you are willing to receive it (the understanding and science of reincarnation) he (John the Baptist) is Elijah who is to come."

As you read these three scriptures you see that the wheels of reincarnation are forever turning. You cannot have reincarnation without karma. Because of karma, reincarnation is active throughout the world.

Many people believe that when they die they will go to heaven and stay forever. This is not the case. When a person dies with a lot of karma, he will be subject to the law of reincarnation, that is, he will be reborn back into the earth to work out his karma again. The Bible says, "But each one is tempted when he is drawn away by his own desires and enticed."

This scripture is very important. It shows that the individual soul with his impressions of past actions, be it drinking, smoking, or gambling is drawn away from heaven back into the earth by his own desires. So if you are in heaven and have a strong desire for cigarettes, then you will be on the next train back to earth. The train is called *reincarnation*.

I can speak of my own personal experience with reincarnation. I was born into a poor family, but one in which I was carefully schooled in the Bible. As an adult, I became heavily involved in drugs and now, here I sit, on Texas Death row. You might ask, "Who would want to come to earth and live a life like that?"

My theory is that, when we are planning our next incarnation, we plan it so that everything that happens to us happens for a very specific reason. There are no accidents. I may seem to most people to be a no-account bum. But I know that I'm a man on a search to find the divine within me and, in this lifetime, my search has led me to Texas Death row, where I live the life of a monk. Not the kind of life a monk would ever dream of, but one in which there is no distraction of monetary things, women, jobs, taxes, cars and I could go on. The temptations of ordinary life are not part of my life and in this way, I am finding my way to self-knowledge and union with God. I think that after I leave this life, I will not lament that I didn't have a great job and drive a Ferrari. I think I will only look at the progress that I made towards union with the divine Self and all other concerns about where I lived and how I died will be of little importance. I will reflect on how I tried to help my fellow man, the mistakes I made and the good things I did. Like all of you, I am here on this earth for only one reason and that is to know God. It may take a long time for us to come to that realization, but all of the things that happen in our lives offer us the opportunity to come closer to God, and this pattern repeats itself over and over again until we reach our final destination.

Questions for personal study:

1. What is the meaning of karma and how does it work in our lives?
2. How is karma in one's life created?
3. What is the connection between karma and reincarnation?
4. How does the cycle of life and death finally come to an end?

Chapter 16 What is Death?

"Just as water (merges) in the ocean, milk in milk, ghee in ghee, the space inside the pot, once the pot is broken, merges into the space outside as the individual soul merges into the Universal soul."

-The Guru Gita

Like many of you, there was a time in my life that I was afraid of death. It is only natural for man to fear the unknown. My fear came about through years of mental conditioning, growing up watching horror movies about the dead coming back to life, haunting people, killing people, only made matters worse to the point I was afraid of funeral homes and grave yards. When my great-grandmother died, I was afraid to go up to the casket to look at her. I really believed that she would rise up and grab me. This was my state of mind. I was young, brainwashed and scared of death.

Professor Pandurangi writes, "To overcome this fear of death, a person must realize that his identity is not confined to his physical body. Even after a person loses his physical body, he continues to exist, for a human being is the eternal Atman, the Self. One must discover this Atman (God) through meditation."

This is true. After embracing the life-giving teachings of the Siddha Yoga path, I can honestly tell you that I do not fear death. I understand that I am not this body, but the eternal Atman. There is no such thing as death for the soul. When this is the case, why do we worry? Why do we weep?

In the Bhagavad Gita it says, "For the soul there is neither birth nor death at any time...He is not slain when the body is slain."

I have spoken with many of my brothers here on Death Row concerning this phenomenon we call death. Many people are afraid and that's understandable. You can see it in their eyes; nobody wants to deal with the subject. Some people crack jokes about death, but behind the laughs there is fear. The fear is strong because many of the brothers identify themselves with being the body. This is a problem within itself. Being attached and holding on to something that's transient always causes pain and sorrow. The fact of the matter is, we will all leave this planet one day, that is, we will have to leave these bodies behind. Swami Sivananda said, "O Man, do not be afraid of death at all." This is a priceless message. Always remember that you are the eternal Atman, and not the body. We are created out of the very nature of God. This is the yogic science that I share with the brothers here. There are some brothers waking up into the knowledge of the Self. It is this knowledge that destroys the fear of death. Tell me, what man is able to destroy the Soul? The soul is never born and it will never die. The Katha Upanishad says, "If the slayer thinks that he kills, and if the slain thinks that he dies, neither knows the ways of truth. The eternal in man cannot kill, the eternal in man cannot die."

It would be wise for the individual to study this phenomenon we call death. For, as death crossing my path, I see, hear and read about it in its many forms every day. Death is all around us, whether we like it nor not. I am able to cope with death because I have knowledge of my own divine Self. I know that I have a body as a vehicle to use while I am here on earth. But I am not this body. I am spirit and soul made in the image of God, and with this understanding I have unlocked it's mystery and taken away its sting.

I am in a unique position. When the execution date comes to a man on death row, he knows the exact time, cause and place of his own death. That is something very few people in this world know. A man who is here has the opportunity to prepare himself for his death. And here, they do it in many different ways depending on their systems of belief. But when the final day comes for an inmate on death row, he usually faces death with stamina and courage. Some of the men are terribly afraid, but they have their brothers encouraging them. In the supreme teaching it says, "When the body falls into weakness on account of old age or disease, even as a mango, fruit, or the fruit of the holy fig tree, is loosened from its stem, so the spirit of man is loosened from the human body and returns by the same way to life, wherefrom he came." Here on Death Row, many of us are still young when we die. For me, Siddha Yoga is my lifeline because I believe with all my heart that death is just a step from one plane of existence to another.

Death is not the end of life.

Questions for personal study:

1. What does death mean to you?
2. Is death the end of life?
3. Can Man kill the Soul? If not, why?
4. Are you afraid of death?
5. When you think about death, do you think of it as a good or bad thing?

Chapter 17 The Yoga of Jesus, Part 1

"Take my yoke upon you and learn from me, for I am gentle and lowly in heart and you will find rest for your souls, for my yoke is easy and my burden is light."

- Jesus

When we study the life of Jesus, it becomes clear that he was a practitioner of yoga and that he taught the science of yoga to his disciples. Reading this, many people will probably disagree with me, especially my Christian brothers, namely because they do not understand the word "yoga" or its meaning.

The word "yoga" means union. It comes from a Sanskrit root "Yuj" which means to join. Jesus said, "Take my yoke upon you". The word "yoke" comes from the Greek root "zeugnumi" which also means union. Yoga is the science that teaches the method of joining or yoking the individual soul back to God. If man was yoked with God, then Jesus would have never come to earth. But thanks to the fall of Man and his misuse of his free will, man separated himself from God; that is, he has become unconscious of his true Self. Shame on man for forgetting.

By forgetting, man has become lawless, cruel, selfish, greedy, vengeful, arrogant and hateful.

In the Bhagavad Gita it states, "When goodness grows weak, when evil increases I make myself a body. In every age, I come back to deliver the holy, to destroy the sin of the sinner, to establish righteousness".

Also, in the Bible John 3:16, "For God so loved the world that he gave his only begotten Son, that whoever believes in him should not perish but have everlasting life".

Why would God send Jesus to save mankind? Because, Jesus was a master teacher of the yogic science, and having the knowledge of the Self, and being one with God qualified him as a savior of mankind. The only difference between Jesus and Man is that Jesus is conscious of his Higher Self and man is unconscious. Jesus knows God, and Man has forgotten God. So Jesus came to save Man when he tells us, "Take my yoke (the teachings of yoga that reconnects the soul of Man in divine union with God) upon you".

Jesus' life and teachings revolves around the four paths of yoga that are mentioned in the Hindu scriptures. *Karma Yoga, Jnana Yoga, Bhakti Yoga*, and *Raja Yoga*. Throughout the

New Testament, you can see Jesus teaching his disciples the four paths of Yoga.

Karma Yoga is the path of work and action. In this yoga, we are not looking for praise or rewards from the work we do. When we volunteer our time and service in helping those who are in need, we are doing it for the Lord. In the Bible Mathew 25:35-40,

(35) "For I was hungry and you gave me food. I was thirsty and you gave me drink, I was a stranger and you took me in."

(36) "I was naked and you clothed me, I was sick and you visited me; I was in prison and you came to me.

(37) "Then the righteous will answer Him, saying, "Lord when did we see you hungry and feed you, or thirsty and give you drink?"

(38) "When did we see you as a stranger and take you in, or naked and clothe you?"

(39) "Or when did we see you sick, or in prison and come to you?"

(40) "And the King will answer and say to them, ' "Assuredly, I say to you, inasmuch as you did it to one of the least of these my brethren you did it to me."

Jnana Yoga is the "yoga of knowledge". It is the path of pure discrimination and self-inquiry.

Who am I? Why am I here? And where am I
going? In the Bible, Matthew 7:7, Jesus said,
"Ask who am I and the revelation will be given
to you, seek the Kingdom of God within
(through meditation) and you will find (the
experience that you and God are one), knock
(chant the name of the Lord - *Om Namah
Shivaya*) and it (*shaktipat diksha initiation*) will
be opened to you."

In the book of Revelation 4:1, it says:
"After these things (asking, seeking and
knocking) I looked and behold: a door standing
open in heaven (the Sahasrara at the crown of
the head)".

Bhakti Yoga is the "yoga of devotion". It is the
path of complete self-surrender and love for
God through prayer, chanting and ritual
worship. In the Bible, Matthew 25:21, Jesus
says, "Enter into the joy of your Lord."

In the book of Hebrew 13:15, Paul says,
"Therefore by him let us continually offer the
sacrifice of praise to God, that is, the fruit of our
lips, giving thanks to his name."

In the Bhagavad Gita it says, "Give me
your whole heart, love and adore me, worship
me always, bow to me only, and you shall find
me: this is my promise who love you dearly."

"Lay down all duties in me, your refuge. Fear no longer, for I will save you from sin and from bondage."

Raja Yoga is the "yoga of meditation". The word *raja*, from its root *raj,* means *royal.* So Raja Yoga is considered the royal path to union of God with Man. Through this path, the individual actually experiences the realization that he and God are one and that the Kingdom of God is within.

In the Bible, John 10:30, "I and my Father are one."

John 12:45, "And he who sees me sees Him (God) who sent me."

John 14:9-11, "He who has seen me has seen the Father, so how can you say, ' "Show us the Father?" ' Do you not believe that I am in the Father and the Father is in me? The words that I speak to you I do not speak on my own authority, but the Father who dwells in me does the work. Believe me that I am in the Father and the Father is in me, or else believe me for the sake of the works themselves."

Raja Yoga is also associated with *Astanga Yoga,* better known as the "eight-limbed yoga". These are:

1. *Yama* - The practice of five moral restraints: nonviolence, abstention from untruth, abstention from stealing, non-covetousness, and abstention from sexual indulgence.

2. *Niyama* - The practice of five observances: purity, contentment, austerity, study of scriptures, and surrender.

3. *Asana* - The postures, to condition the body for meditation.

4. *Pranayama* - The regulation and restraint of the breath.

5. *Pratyahara* - The withdrawal of the mind from sense objects.

6. *Dharana* - The concentration, fixing the mind on an object or place of contemplation.

7. *Dhyana* - Meditation

8. *Samadhi* - The complete absorption or identification with the object of meditation, meditative union with the Absolute.

Jesus is one with God. This is the yogic science that is the root, or the foundation, of every religion. To be Christ-like is to apply the yogic science that Jesus taught.

In my experience as a seeker and lover of God, I practice all four of the paths to yoga, with raja yoga, the yoga of meditation, being my preferred practice. If you are an active person, then you might want to focus your life on karma yoga, the yoga of action and purpose dedicating all of your actions to God. Different types of people come to know God in different ways. You are not a square peg trying to fit yourself into a round hole. Choose your path of yogic action and walk your own unique path to the knowledge of God.

Questions for personal study:

1. What does yoga mean to you?
2. Do you believe that Jesus practiced yoga?
3. What is the yogic science Jesus taught?
4. What are the four paths of yoga?
5. Which one of the four paths most appeals to you?

Chapter 18 The Yoga of Jesus, Part 2

"For what will it profit a man if he gains the whole world, and loses his own soul? Or what will a man give in exchange for his soul?"

- Jesus

    In this teaching we are going to take a closer look at the two questions Jesus posed to his disciples concerning the individual soul, and the world. We will also look at three stories that illustrate the two questions Jesus posed to his disciples.

    The first question is, "What man in his right mind would sell his infinite soul for a finite world?" The message Jesus is bringing home is that the soul is infinite, unlike the finite world that is transitory, in constant flux. The soul is everlasting and eternal, made in the image and likeness of God, unlimited, unbound and omnipotent. There is no profit or anything to gain in a finite world that's impermanent, existing for a limited time only.

    Let's now look at the first story of Nachiketas found the in the *Katha Upanishad*. Nachiketas was a pure soul, a Brahmin seeking the higher knowledge of life and death from

Lord Yama. In the story, Nachiketas, like Jesus, is being tempted by Lord Yama with worldly possessions. Basically, Lord Yama is asking Nachiketas to sell his infinite soul for a finite world. Here is the dialogue between; Lord Yama and Nachiketas.

Lord Yama: Take horses and gold and cattle and elephants; choose sons and grandsons that shall live a hundred years. Have vast expanses of land and live as many years as you desire. Or choose another gift that you think equal to this, and enjoy it with wealth and long life. Be a ruler of this vast earth. I will grant you all your desires. Ask for any wishes in the World of Mortals, however hard to obtain. To attend on you, I will give you fair maidens with chariots and musical instruments. But ask me not, Nachiketas, the secrets of Death."

Nachiketas: "All these pleasures pass away, o End of All! They weaken the power of life. And indeed, how short is all life! Keep thee thy horses and dancing and singing. Man cannot be satisfied with wealth. Shall we enjoy wealth with you in sight? Shall we live whilst you are in power? I can only ask for the boon I have asked. When a mortal here on earth has felt his own immortality, could he wish for a long life of pleasures, for the lust of deceitful beauty? Solve then the doubt as to the great beyond.

Grant me the gift that unveils the mystery. This is the only gift Nachiketas can ask".

Nachiketas is steadfast and rejects Lord Yama's offer of worldly possessions. In the Bible, the devil tempts Jesus by showing him all the kingdoms of the world in a moment of time. Like, Nachiketas, Jesus is steadfast and rejects the devil's offer.

Lord Yama: "There is the Path of Joy, and there is the Path of Pleasure. Both attract the soul. Who follows the first comes to good; who follows pleasure reaches not the end. The two paths lie in front of Man. Pondering on them, the wise man chooses the Path of Joy, the fool takes the Path of Pleasure. You have pondered, Nachiketas, on pleasures and you have rejected them. You have not accepted that chain of possessions wherewith men bind themselves and beneath which they sink.

There is the Path of Wisdom and the Path of Ignorance. They are far apart and lead to different ends. You are, Nachiketas, a follower of the Path of Wisdom, many pleasures tempt you not. Abiding in the midst of ignorance, thinking themselves wise and learned, fools go aimlessly hither and thither, like blind led by the blind. What lies beyond life shines not to those who are childish or careless, or deluded by wealth. This is the only world, there is no other, they say, and thus they go from death to death."

Lord Yam is pleased that Nachiketas rejected the finite things of the world, and grants Nachiketas' wish by teaching him the mysteries and knowledge of life and death. When Lord Yama speaks of the Path of Joy, he is speaking about the infinite, everlasting joy that is felt and experienced in meditation, when the individual turns within and meditates on God. Psalms 39:9 "And my soul shall be joyful in the Lord, it shall rejoice in his salvation." The pleasures of the world only bring pain and suffering. This is the point Jesus was making to his disciples asking them to use discrimination between the real infinite soul and the unreal finite world.

Our second story deals with King Solomon. As we know, Solomon was the king of Jerusalem, and very wealthy. He was also known for his wisdom. You will see in this story that everything Nachiketas renounced, Solomon accumulated and built for himself. On the other hand, Solomon had what Nachiketas was seeking - wisdom and understanding. In the book of Ecclesiastes, 2:1,3,7,8,10,11:

2:1 "I said in mine heart, go to now, I will prove thee with mirth; therefore, enjoy pleasure and behold, this also is vanity.

2:3 "I sought in mine heart to give myself unto wine yet acquainting mine heart with wisdom, and to lay hold on folly, till I might see what was that good for the Sons of Men, which they should do under the heaven all the days of their life."

2:7 "I got me servants and maidens, and had servants born in my house; also, I had great possessions of great and small cattle above all that were in Jerusalem before me."

2:8 "I gathered me also silver and gold, and the peculiar treasure of kinds and of the provinces. I got me men singers and women singers, and the delights of the Sons of Men, as musical instruments and that of all sorts."

2:10 "And whatsoever mine eyes desired I kept not from them, I withheld not my heart from any joy; for my heart rejoiced in all my labor and this was my portion of all my labor."

2:11 "Then I looked on all the works that my hands had labored to do, and behold, all was vanity and vexation of spirit, and there was no profit under the sun."

Solomon makes a conscious choice in his heart (mind) to "go to now" and enjoy pleasure. Whereas, Lord Yama taught Nachiketas that whoever follows the Path of Pleasure reaches not the end. Also, we see Solomon looking into his heart to drink wine and study wisdom, and to lay hold on folly. Folly means "to be silly or foolish". Solomon wanted to see and experience the things the Sons of Men were doing under the sun. Remember the mind follows the pull of the senses. Solomon said, "Whatsoever mine eyes desired, I kept not from them". These desires are a reflection of the heart and mind. Solomon answers Jesus' questions when he says, "All was vanity and vexation of spirit, and there was not profit under the sun". The word vanity specifically means "to lead astray, something transitory and unsatisfactory, or existing only briefly". Vanity is another name for Maya, the cosmic illusion that veils reality.

We now look at Jesus' second question to his disciples, "What will a man give in exchange for his soul?" or, "What are you willing to sacrifice to save yourself?" By taking up the yoke of Jesus, the Yogic Science, you can become your own savior.

Our last story deals with the rich man in the Bible, Matthew 19:16-22:

19:16 Now behold, one come and said to Him, "Good teacher, what good thing shall I do that I may have eternal life?"

19:17 "So he said to him, 'Why do you call me good?' No one is good but one, that is, God. But if you want to enter into life, keep the Commandments."

19:18 "He said to Him, 'Which ones?' and Jesus said, 'You shall not murder, you shall not commit adultery, you shall not steal, you shall not bear false witness'."

19:19 "Honor your Father and your Mother, and you shall love your neighbor as yourself."

19:20 "The young man said to Him, 'All these things I have kept from my youth. What do I still lack?'"

19:21 "Jesus said to him, 'If you want to be perfect, go sell what you have and give to the poor, and you will have treasure in heaven, and come, follow me.'"

19:22 "But when the young man heard that saying, he went away sorrowful, for he had great possessions."

The rich man had the keys to heaven but he made a poor choice by rejecting eternal life, which is infinite and everlasting for the finite things of the world. However his question to

Jesus is very important. It shows every human being deep down inside consciously or unconsciously has a sincere desire to reconnect with God. The rich man told Jesus that he had kept all the commandments and was wondering what he still lacked. Jesus told him if he wanted to be perfect to go sell all he had and give to the poor, and he would have treasure in heaven. To be perfect means to be complete. Jesus saw that the rich man was incomplete by hoarding all his riches on earth. The rich man walked away sorrowful with a broken heart. Just the idea of him giving all his possessions to poor people hurt him. This sorrow comes from his attachment to worldly things. That is why Jesus said it would be hard for a rich man to enter the Kingdom of Heaven.

The rich man or worldly -minded man is addicted to the finite world, chasing after things that will never bring peace and joy, but rather hardship and pain. The man who refuses to let go of the world will never enter into Heaven.

Here on Death Row, no one made the choice to give up worldly possessions or loved ones or material possessions. On the outside, some of us were very wealthy and some even famous, or I should say *infamous*. Once we entered these walls, we said goodbye to the outside world, to the trappings of life. We did not consciously choose to do this; rather, the choice was made for us. Still, the result has been the same. Over time, every one of us here has had to let go of the events and possessions of the outside world. Some of us have watched our children grow up and go to prison themselves, and we could do nothing to stop it from behind these bars. We've seen our loved ones get sick and die without the opportunity to say goodbye. The world had changed all around us, but for those of us in here, the world changes very little. So I've come to be attached to the only attachment that means anything at all - the attachment to God and to knowing that God dwells within me, as me. This is where my happiness and enthusiasm for life comes from. This is what gives me peace and contentment.

Questions for personal study:

1. What message is Jesus teaching us concerning the Soul?
2. Why did Nachiketas reject Lord Yama's offer?
3. What was Nachiketas asking for?
4. Why did Jesus tell the rich man to sell his possessions?
5. Had the rich man sold his possessions, what do you think he would have gained?

Chapter 19 The Yoga of Jesus, Part 3

"When you lift up the Son of Man, then you will know that I am He."

- Jesus

Who or what is the Son of Man, and how do we lift him up? In the Bible, there are several passages in the New Testament where Jesus talks about the *Son of Man*. In many of these passages, Jesus is referring to himself indirectly as the Son of Man. In the book of Mark 14:41, Jesus says to his disciples, "The hour has come behold, the Son of Man is being betrayed into the hands of sinners." We know that Jesus is the Son of Man, and that he was betrayed by Judas. However, the Son of Man in this case represents the physical body, born out of the union between man and woman. Every human being is a *Son of Man* and has the potential to become a *Son of God* here on earth. When Jesus said, "When you life up the Son of Man", none of his disciples made any attempt to physically life him up off the ground. Had they done so, he would have admonished them.

Lifting up the Son of Man means rising above the lower Self, the body consciousness, transcending the ego-mind of *I, me,* and *mine* and becoming detached from the sense identification with the body, thus turning the life force back, making it flow up towards the higher Self. Over a lifetime, we waste the powerful life force through spending it on sense pleasures. Eventually, we become old and worn out because the life force has been squandered on useless pursuits.   The life force is the *kundalini shakti* that lies dormant at the base of the spine in the *muladhara chakra.* When the disciple receives shaktipat, the kundalini begins to unfold and travel upwards through the spine, the *sushumna nadi*, until it reaches the *sahasrara* at the crown of the head. When this happens Jesus says to his disciples, "Then you will know that I am He." The knowing takes place within the disciples when he experiences the *samadhi* state and learns that he and God are one, and that he and Jesus share the same Christ - nature. He then begins to see this oneness in everyone he sees and he is uplifted.

Through meditation we are able to raise the Son of Man from the lower self, to the higher self by focusing our attention on the *ajna chakra* between the eyebrows. Attention is the ability or power to concentrate mentally, carefully observing or listening. When we concentrate on the *ajna chakra*, we repeat verbally or mentally the syllable OM (sometimes written as AUM) which is the primordial sound and the original divine sound of the universe. In the *Kaivalyopanishad*, it says: "Meditate on the highest Lord allied to Uma (the power of divine will, Shiva Shakti), powerful, three-eyed, blue-necked, and tranquil." This is Lord Shiva in his effulgence. The holy man (the disciple on the path) reaches Him who is the Source of All, the witness (the Atman that is ever-present) of all and is beyond darkness."

Why is it so hard to lift up the Son of Man? The Son of Man is not hard to lift up. However, we live in a time and age of Kali Yuga (the dark age) where many people are spiritually drunk, and have become materialistic and worldly-minded. These people identify with their lower self and in doing so, they have become attached to the body.

In the book of Romans 8:5-8, Paul says:

5. For those who live according to the flesh, their minds are on the things of the flesh, but those who live according to the Spirit, their mind dwells on the things of the Spirit.

6. For to be carnally-minded is death, but to be spiritually-minded is life and peace.

7. Because the carnal mind is enmity against God, for it is not subject to the law of God, nor indeed can be.

8. So then, those who are in the flesh cannot please God.

In these teachings, we have learned that it is important to raise the Son of Man. If you are not willing to raise the Son of Man, then you can never say you know Jesus. And so, this is why Jesus taught this yogic science to his disciples so that they may know him.

Can the *Son of Man* be lifted up here on Texas Death Row? Can a place of violence and hatred be transformed into paradise? Individually, one-by-one, we transform our experience of life into a vision of paradise as we come to know that God dwells within each one of us. He did not forget about the murderers and criminals. We are all included and the hope of peace and redemption is within each of us. The transformation starts with the choice we make in each moment. Will your next thought be one of separation or one of unity? I can live in the most desolate and isolated place on earth and still be the happiest man on earth, if I know who I really am.

Questions for personal study:

1. Who is the Son of Man and how do you lift him up?
2. What is the life force?
3. How is the shakti related to the life force?
4. Where is the Ajna chakra located?
5. As the Son of Man, what do you do in your own life to uplift yourself and others around you?

Chapter 20 The Reality of God

"The Self is Brahman, the Absolute, the Supreme transcendent Reality."

- *Atharva Veda*

Brahman, the most high God is one, without beginning or end. The Supreme Being, the Supreme Reality, the All in All, the everlasting God, the Supreme Consciousness, the Divine Intelligence, the innermost Self manifesting everywhere is all beings. He is God, omnipresent; He is God, omniscient; He is God, omnipotent. He is beyond north, south, east and west, beyond what is above or below, the creator of the heavens and earth, the eternal in Man.

The question is frequently ask to me, "How do you know God exists if you've never seen him?" This is a very good questions that deserves a good answer. I will answer this question with an illustration. A man and his family drove to the mall to do a little Christmas shopping. They stayed in the mall for six hours shopping . After shopping, they left the mall, but there is one problem. The man can't remember where he parked his car. Now, because he can't remember where he parked his car does not mean that his car doesn't exist. No, it only means that he can't remember. It's the same if a person loses his keys in his house. He said, "I can't find my keys. I set them down and now I can't find them." Does that mean that his keys don't exist? No, it only means he can't remember where the keys are. The keys, like the car, exist, they are present, it's just that men have a tendency to forget. Today, people are saying, "I don't believe in God." Basically what they are saying is "I can't remember God". They will never remember until they turn within and discover God for themselves.

The scriptures say Man knows nothing until he labors, and until he labors, he'll never know. The laboring means turning within, seeking and asking the question, "Who am I?" This is self-inquiry. If you don't inquire about your own Self, you will never know God. The man who can't remember where he parked his car will never find it until he makes an effort to search for it, until he begins to inquire within himself. When the car is found, the search is over.

The proof of God which many people reject today can be experienced within themselves. God dwells in Man in the form of the Atman, Divine Consciousness. The scriptures say, "In the union with Him is the supreme proof of his reality". The proof is in the nature of God which is *sat-chit-ananda. Sat* means existence. *Chit* means consciousness, and *ananda* means bliss. God is *sat*, he is self-existing. There never was a time when God was not. God has always been, and will forever be the Supreme Reality. The *Katha Upanishads* says, "In the faith of 'He is' his existence must be perceived, and he must be perceived in his essence. When He is perceived as 'He is', then shines forth the revelation of his essence." God is *chit*; he is Supreme Consciousness and he is conscious of the Self. Man is created out of Supreme Consciousness; therefore, he is conscious of the Self. Man knows that he exists. How does he know he exists? It is due to consciousness which is also light. Jesus said, "I am the light of the world. Jesus was aware of himself being a part of God which is *chit*-consciousness. The *Maitri Upanishad* says, "There is a spirit who is amongst the things of this world and yet he is above the things of this world. He is clear and pure, in the peace of a void of vastness. He is beyond the life of the body and the mind, ever born, never -dying, everlasting, ever one in his own greatness. He is the Spirit whose power gives consciousness to the body; he is the driver of the Chariot." *Chit* is omnipresence; it is the divine intelligence in the universe, the Atman in Man. Life itself is consciousness. The reality of God is the breath of Man. The Bible says that God blew his own breath into man and man became a living (conscious) soul. God is *ananda*; he is supreme bliss. The scriptures says that God is love. The love of God is felt in deep meditation on the heart. Man is also created out of love. You love your mother, wife and kids. Because of God who dwells in you as bliss, you are able to share and express this love. God is *sat-chit-ananda*. He exists because he is.

There is a story in the *Chandogya Upanishad* that best illustrates the reality of God. *Om*. There lived once a boy, Svetaketu Aruneya, by name. One day his father spoke to him in this way: "Svetaketu, go and become a student of sacred wisdom. There is no one in our family who has not studied the holy Vedas and who might only be given the name of Brahman by courtesy."

The boy left at the age of twelve and, having learnt the Vedas, he returned home at the age of twenty-four, very proud of his learning and having a great opinion of himself. His father, observing this, said to him, "Svetaketu, my boy, you seem to have a great opinion of yourself. You think you are learned and you are proud. Have you asked for that knowledge whereby what is not heard is heard, what is not thought is thought, and what is not known is known?"

"What is that knowledge, Father?", asked Svetaketu.

"Just by knowing a lump of clay, my son, all that is clay can be known, since any differences are only words and the reality is clay, just as by knowing a piece of gold, that is gold can be known, since any differences are only words and the reality is only gold. And just as by knowing a piece of iron, all that is iron is known, since any differences are only words and the reality is only iron."

Svetaketu said, "Certainly my honored masters knew not this themselves. If they had known, why would they not have told me? Explain this to me, Father."

"So be it my child." And a dialogue began:

-Bring me a fruit from this banyan tree.

- Here it is, Father.

-Break it.

-It is broken, Sir.

-What do you see in it?

-Very small seeds, sir.

-Break one of them, my son.

-It is broken, sir.

-What do you see in it?

-Nothing at all, sir.

-My son, from the very essence in the seed which you cannot see comes in truth this vast banyan tree. Believe me, my son, an invisible and subtle essence is the Spirit of the whole universe. That is reality. That is the Atman. Thou art That."

-Explain more to me, Father

-So be it, my son. Place this salt in water and come to me tomorrow morning.

Svetaketu did as he was commanded, and in the morning, his father said to him, "

-Bring me the salt you put into the water last night.

Svetaketu looked into the water, but could not find it, for it had dissolved.

His father then said, "Taste the water from this side. How is it?"

-It is salt.

-Taste it from that side. How is it?

-It is salt.

-Look for the salt again and come again to me.

-I cannot see the salt. I only see water.

-In the same way, oh my son, you cannot see the Spirit. But in truth he is here. An invisible and subtle essence is the Spirit of the whole universe. That is reality. That is Truth. Thou art That."

Svetaketu then said, "Explain more to me, Father."

-So be it, my son.

-Even as a man, oh my son, who had been led blindfolded from his land of the Gandharas and then left in a desert place, might wander to the East and North and South, because he had been taken blindfolded and left in an unknown place, but if a good man took off his bandage and told him, "In that direction is the land of the Gandharas, go in that direction";then, if he were a wise man, he would go asking from village to village until he would have reached his land of the Gandharas. So it happens, in this world to a man who has a Master to direct him to the land of the Spirit. Such a man can say, "I shall wander in this world until I attain liberation, but then I shall go and reach my home. " This invisible and subtle essence if the Spirit of the whole universe. That is Reality. That is Truth. Thou art That." And the dialogue ended.

What is "That"? And how can we know That for ourselves? That is Brahman, the Supreme Consciousness, the Spirit in Man. Brahman is the creator of the universe. The world we live in is created out of That. The reality of God exists in the seen and the unseen. From the unseen which is that formless Brahman, comes the seen, the world. The world exists because the world was created out of That. The Father said to his son, "This invisible and subtle essence is the Spirit of the whole universe". In the Bible, Hebrews 11:3, it says, "By faith we understand that the worlds were framed by the word of God, so that the things which are seen were not made of things which are visible." In the story, the father said to his son, "My son, you cannot see the Spirit but in truth, he is here." In the Upanishads it says, "The truth of the Atman must be heard about, reasoned upon, and meditated upon." What this means is that you must hear the truth with your spiritual ears. Jesus said, "Let those who have ears to hear, let them hear." Not with the physical ears; rather, he is talking about the spiritual ears. If you listen with your physical earns, you will always reject the Truth. After hearing the truth, you must reflect on it. The truth can be tested, so don't take my word for it; try it for yourself. By reflecting on the truth, turn within and meditate on your own divine Self. In the Bhagavad Gita 18:55, it says, "By love (devotion), he (the yogi) knows me in truth (he who worships God, must worship in Spirit in truth) who I am and what I am. And when he knows (experiences) me in truth, he enter (merges, becomes one) into my Being." When the individual through meditation becomes one with God, he will be able to proclaim, "I am That!"

In the Bible, we have read about very profound experiences of God that provide proof that he really exists. A big booming voice comes out of nowhere, or a huge angel appears. And so, as human beings, we are waiting for these signs as proof that God is real. What we don't understand is that God is everywhere, in everything. You don't have to look very far to find God. The nature of God is pure love and where ever you see evidence of pure love, there you see the face of God. There is pure love on Texas Death Row, in the way the men support each other when they are facing their day of execution. There is pure love on death row when one man speaks sweetly to another in the midst of so much chaos. There is pure love on death row when I sit for meditation and am filled with divine light, contentment and peace.

You don't have to look very far for God. Look into the face of a child or a dog who welcomes you home. God exists in the virtues - in acts of simple kindness. If you don't like what you see in the world, Baba Muktananda tells us to change the prescription of our glasses-choose to see the world differently. Choose to see God.

Questions for personal study:

1. Do you believe in God?
2. If yes, what is your personal proof that God exists?
3. What is the nature of God?
4. How can we experience God?

Chapter 21 The Crucifixion and Resurrection of the Soul

"I am the resurrection and the life; he that believes in me, though he were dead, yet shall he live."

-Jesus

In Part One of the chapter on the Yoga of Jesus, I explain that yoga is the science that teaches the method of joining or yoking the individual soul back with God. If we keep this in mind, it will be easy for you to understand the crucifixion and resurrection of the soul. You are probably wondering, "What is the connection?" The answer is *everything*.

The crucifixion and resurrection are highly symbolic. It is a universal science that has been taught for thousands of years around the world by many different cultures although in the Christian tradition, this story is only 2,000 years old. In each culture, there is a story about someone dying and coming back to life to save mankind and the world . The greatest story ever told is found in the Bible detailing the life of Jesus. Jesus was crucified on the cross and in three days, he rose from the grave.

This is the basic story that everybody is familiar with; however, there is a deeper meaning behind this story. But before we're able to explore the hidden meaning of its symbols, you have to understand that the world we live in is full of signs and symbols and that everything is and isn't at the same time. I have listed two definitions below, so that you will be able to understand this teaching clearly.

The definition for *crucify* is "to put a person to death by nailing or binding to a cross. To mortify or subdue (the flesh). To treat cruelly, torment. Latin, 'to attach'."

The definition for *resurrection* is "the act of rising from the dead or returning to life. The state of those who have returned to life. The act of bringing back to practice, notice, or use, revival. Latin, 'to rise again'."

In the Qur'an it says, "We explain the signs by various symbols", and also "And how many signs in the heavens and the earth do they pass by? Yet they turn their faces away from them."

When we hear the word *crucifixion*, the first thing that comes to mind is Jesus on the cross. However, Jesus is only a symbolic representation of you, the individual soul, that has taken on a body, and has become attached to the cross. The cross represents the physical world of time and space (finite and limited). When the Soul identifies with the body, and forgets its true identity, Man becomes attached or crucified on the cross.

The word *resurrection* means rising from the dead or returning to life, not the physical dead, but the mental dead. The resurrection is not a future even- it's happening now! In the Bible, Paul says, "Even when we were dead (mentally) in trespasses (disobeying and committing sin), the experience of God made us alive (conscious) together with Christ and raised (from the lower self) us up together and made us sit together in the heavenly places in Christ Jesus."

The resurrection takes place when the Soul begins to remember its true nature (higher Self) and detach itself from the cross, and begins to move away from identifying with the body.

The story of the *Prodigal Son* also deals with the crucifixion and resurrections of the Soul. In the book of Luke, Chapter 15 (various verses), Jesus taught this story to the sinners and Pharisees.

Verse 11 - Then he said, "A certain man (God) had two sons (souls).

Verse 12 - And the younger of them said to his father, "Father give me the portion of goods (free will, knowledge, wisdom and understanding) that falls to me. So He (God) divided (gave equal power) to them (souls) his livelihood (all powers).

Verse 13 - And not many days after, the younger son gathered it all together, journeyed (separated himself from God) to a far country and there wasted his possessions (free will, knowledge, wisdom and understanding) with prodigal living.

Verse 14 - But when he (the soul) had spent them all, (realized he was spiritually bankrupt) there arose a severe famine (a spiritual hunger) in that land (body/temple) and he began to be in want (a desire to reconnect with God).

Verse 24- For this my son (made in my image) was dead (mentally) and alive (made conscious through the mental resurrection). Again, he was lost (unconscious) and is found (has the knowledge of the Self). And they began to be merry (in spiritual bliss).

The story of the *Prodigal Son* is the story of every human being on the planet earth. The story also sheds light concerning the second coming of Jesus. For the last two thousand years, people have been waiting on Jesus to come back. However, the only person that has to come back is you! Coming back means remembering, waking up into the knowledge of the Self, the realization that you and God are one. The scriptures speak the truth when we reflect on Verse 24. When the individual soul comes back to God, he will be able to say in the words of Jesus, "I am the resurrection."

Sometimes, you hear people talking about the "second coming of Christ", that time in which there will be a reckoning of sins. But what we are all waiting for is for Christ to return to us in our own hearts. That is the second coming. At one time, you knew who you were. You knew that God dwelled within you as you and you looked on your fellow-man as God. Then, through numerous lifetimes of lust and attachment to materials, you came to forget your true nature and began to look on yourself and others as separate from God. You came to think that you must covet what is yours and protect what you have from others. But deep down inside of you, the knowledge of who you are has never left you. It remains inside of you, waiting. Sometimes poverty, bad fortune or disease causes us to stop and take a good look at the things that are important in life - love and harmony with yourself and others. And in those times, you abandon the quest for fame, money and power in order to align yourself with your highest virtues. In those moments, you are experiencing your own resurrection. Know that the crucifixion and the resurrection are events that can happen.....just like that!....within your own being.

Questions for personal study:

1. What is the resurrection?
2. When does the resurrection take place?
3. What is the meaning of the cross?
4. Who is the *prodigal son*?
5. What is the meaning of being lost?

Chapter 22 The Origin of the Ego

"The individual Self, deluded by forgetfulness of his identity with the Divine Self, bewildered by his ego, grieves and is sad. But when he recognizes the worshipful Lord as his own true Self, and beholds his glory, he grieves no more."

- Mandaka Upanishad

What is the ego? The ego is the pseudo soul. *Pseudo* means false or deceptive. The ego is the unconscious soul that interprets everything in terms of I, me and mine. The ego is, "I am". For example, "I am a man, I am a woman, I am a boy" and so on. The ego is the false personality, the dark mask of ignorance that covers the soul's ability to discriminate between the real and the unreal.

The diagram on the next page shows the characteristics of the ego as opposed to the characteristics of the Divine Self. It is said that the lower self, the body of desires, is distorted by the dark ethers of the flesh. When the soul identifies with the body, it becomes distorted or twisted from its natural God-state. The distortion takes place when the soul moves away from consciousness. It is the equivalent of a person walking around in a waking sleep.

If you have ever taken a course in chemistry in school, then you should be familiar with the transmutation process of solids, liquids and gasses. The diagram below shows the transmutation and descent of the soul from its natural God-state to an unnatural state. The diagram also represents the seven chakras. The top of the diagram represents the higher Self, heaven, light consciousness, pure thoughts, positive, "I am God", son of God, soul-oneness and love. The bottom of the diagram represents the lower Self, hell, darkness , unconsciousness, impure thoughts, negative, I am man, son of man-soul in a body, duality and hate. This is where the kundalini energy lies sleeping, waiting for the bestowal of *shaktipat*, the spiritual awakening from a true Master.

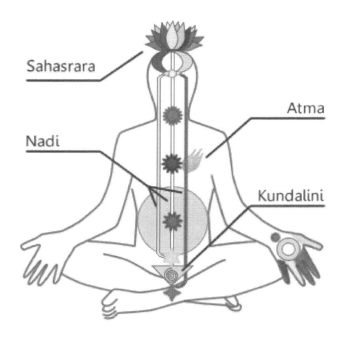

In the Qur'an it says, "If anyone withdraws himself from the remembrance of Allah (God) most gracious, we appoint for him an evil one, to be an intimate companion to him. Such evil ones really hinder them from the path, but they think that they are being guided aright."

The withdrawal and separation from the remembrance of Allah (Supreme Consciousness) is the root cause of man's pain and suffering here on earth. The evil one is present in man under the name ego. When the individual soul becomes spellbound by *maya* (desire), it becomes unconscious and gives birth or life to the ego. The Qur'an says that the evil one is an intimate companion to Man, preventing Man from progressing on the spiritual path; and all this while, Man believes that he is on the right path.

The ego is plagued by six faults that man has to overcome. These faults are: lust, anger, greed, delusion, pride and envy. They are the fetters that bind the soul to the body. A list of the six faults are defined below.

1. *Lust.* Intense or unrestrained sexual craving. An overwhelming desire or craving, a lust for power. To have an intense or obsessive desire.

2. *Anger.* A feeling of extreme displeasure, hostility, indignation, or exasperation toward someone or something.

3. *Greed.* An excessive desire to acquire or possess, as wealth or power, beyond what one needs or deserves.

4. *Delusion.* The act or process of deluding, deception, something that is false disseminated

or believed, a false belief held in spite of invalidating evidence, as a condition of certain forms of mental illness.

5. *Pride*. Pleasure or satisfaction taken in one's work, achievements or possessions.

6. *Envy*. A feeling of discontent and resentment aroused by another's desirable possessions or qualities, accompanied by a strong desire to have them for oneself.

Sometimes more than one of these faults will be operating at the same time. A man who is *proud* of his possessions is under the *delusion* that they will last forever. A wise man may own these same possessions, but he realizes that , like everything in this world, they will pass away. What looks beautiful today may not look so beautiful down the line.

On death row, even though we live with few possessions, we still live with the six faults on a moment-to-moment basis. For some of the inmates, they are so steeped in these faults, that the only relief they get is when they are asleep. For them, it doesn't matter whether they are here on the inside or out there enjoying all that life offers in the way of material goods. They still live with these faults in every thought they have. Thoughts of lust, greed, pride and anger follow them everywhere they go. So for them, it doesn't matter where they live because truthfully, they live in only one place and that place is in the hell they create for themselves.

By meditating on the higher Self, chanting and reading the holy scriptures, Man creates the fire of yoga within his own body, by which the six faults are burned away, thus allowing Man to rise above the ego and reconnect with God. When one follows the consistent daily practice of meditation, slowly but surely, these faults lose their power over Man and eventually let go of him completely, so that he is able to live a life of spiritual freedom, loving all that he sees through the eyes of divine wisdom. That's how Texas Death Row can become a paradise for those who are willing to open their eyes to the truth of life.

Questions for personal study:
1. What is the origin of ego?
2. Is the ego separate from the soul?
3. What happens when the soul forgets its true nature?
4. What binds the soul to the body?
5. How is yoga of fire created?

Chapter 23 The Four Gatekeepers

"But do you want to know, oh foolish Man, that faith without works (effort) is dead?"

-St. James

"Salvation is accomplished through the efforts of the individual. There is no mediator between Man and his salvation."

-Ancient Egyptian Proverbs

The purpose of life here on earth is self-realization. In essence, self-realization means liberation or salvation from the cycle of birth and death. When the cycle is broken, Man becomes a *jivanmukta*, one who is liberated in this very life.

The *Yoga Vasishtha* is a Sanskrit text written around the twelfth century that deals with the nature of the mind. In it, the Sage Vasishtha instructs Lord Rama about the nature and control of the mind and the way to liberation. In the second chapter, "On the Behavior of the Seeker", the Sage Vasishtha teaches Lord Rama about the *four gate keepers*. The four gate keepers represent the four paths to liberation. Liberation or salvation does not come without self-effort. With this understanding , we can apply these teachings to our everyday life.

The Sage Vasishtha says:

"*Self-control* (the first gate keeper), oh Rama, is the best remedy for all physical and mental ills. When there is self-control, even the food you eat tastes better. Otherwise, it tastes bitter. He who wears the armor of self-control is not harmed by sorrow. He who even while hearing, touching, seeing, smelling and tasting what is regarded as pleasant and unpleasant, is neither elated nor depressed - he is self-controlled. He who looks upon all beings with equal vision, having brought under control the sensations of pleasure and pain, is self-controlled. He who, though living amongst all is unaffected by them, neither feels elated nor hates, is self-controlled.

Inquiry, the second gate keeper to liberation, should be undertaken by an intelligence that has been purified by a close study of the scriptures, and this inquiry should be unbroken. By such inquiry, the intelligence becomes deep and is able to realize the Supreme; hence inquiry alone is the best remedy for the long-lasting illness known as *samsara*, attachment to the material world.

The wise man regards strength, intellect, efficiency and timely action as the fruits of inquiry. Indeed, kingdom, prosperity and enjoyment as well as final liberation, are all the fruits of inquiry. The spirit of inquiry protects one from the calamities that befall the unthinking fool. When the mind has been rendered dull by the absence of inquiry, even the cool rays of the moon turn into deadly weapons and the childish imagination throws up a goblin in every dark spot. Hence, the non-inquiring fool is really a storehouse of sorrow. It is the absence of inquiry that gives rise to actions that are harmful to oneself and to others and to numerous psychosomatic illnesses. Therefore, one should avoid the company of such unthinking people.

Contentment is the third gate keeper to liberation. He who has quaffed the nectar of contentment does not relish craving for sense pleasures. No delight in this world is as sweet as contentment, which destroys all sins.

What is contentment? To renounce all craving for what is not obtained unsought and to be satisfied with what comes unsought, without being elated or depressed even by them - this is contentment. As one is not satisfied in the Self, he will be subjected to sorrow. With the rise of contentment, the purity of one's heart blooms.

The contented man who possesses nothing owns the world.

Satsanga (the company of wise, holy and enlightened persons) is yet another gate keeper to liberation. Satsanga enlarges one's intelligence and destroys one's ignorance and one's psychological distress. Whatever be the cost, however difficult it may be, whatever obstacles may stand in its way, satsanga should never be neglected. For satsanga alone is one's light on the path of life. Satsanga is indeed superior to all other forms of religious practices like charity, austerity, pilgrimage and the performance of religious rites.

One should, by every means in one's power, adore and serve the holy men who have realized the truth and in whose heart the darkness of ignorance has been dispelled. They, on the other hand, who treat such holy men disrespectfully, surely invite great suffering.

These four gatekeepers- contentment, satsanga (the company of wise men), the spirit of inquiry, and self-control - are the four surest means by which those who are drowning in this ocean of *samskaras* (repetitive history) can be saved. Contentment is the supreme gain. Satsanga is the best companion to the destination. The spirit of inquiry itself is the greatest wisdom. And, self-control is supreme happiness. If you are unable to maintain all these four, then practice one; by diligent practice of one of these, the others will makes themselves known to you."

To acquire the presence of the four gate keepers in your life may seem like an impossible task. But really, it is very simple. Dedicate each action to God. When one pauses before any new activity and silently dedicates that action to God, then the four gate keepers rise up within him. Self-control asserts itself by showing him which action to take, inquiry rises up as he becomes fascinated by the beauty of the present moment, the satsanga of his own great company reveals itself, and from this arises the state of contentment.

> This is a great practice. With each new action, pause and say silently to yourself, "I __(action)__ to have a vision of God within." These are the words that my Guru taught to me and from this teaching, my life has changed.

Here are a few examples:

- I take a shower to have a vision of God within. Taking a shower is a great event!"
- I speak to my boss to have a vision of God within. Speaking to my boss is a great event!"
- I sit in traffic to have a vision of God within. Sitting in traffic is a great event!
- I play with my children to have a vision of God within. Playing with my children is a great event!

When you start a new activity, pause for a moment and repeat these words. You will activate the four gate keepers and you will experience a divine difference in your life!

Questions for personal study:

1. What is it that we must become liberated from?
2. What was the teaching to Lord Rama?
3. What are the names of the four gate keepers?
4. Who is self-controlled?
5. What is satsanga? Why is it important?

Chapter 24 Yogic Diet

And God said, "Behold, I have given you every herb-bearing seed, which is upon the face of all the earth, and every tree, in which is the fruit of a tree yielding seed, to you it shall be for meat".

-The Bible

What is the proper diet for a human being? What kind of food should we eat to maintain health in the body? And what foods should we avoid? There are many books on health and many diets a person can choose from. I believe the best diet is the yogic diet, as described in the scriptures of the Bible and the Bhagavad Gita.

First, let me say that I am not a vegetarian. However, I would love to become a vegetarian and eat fresh vegetables and fruits every day. However, due to my circumstances here on Death Row, I don't have access to very much nutritious food. As a matter of fact, there is nothing fresh when it comes to food here on Death Row, and many inmates can testify to that. Our meals consist mostly of raw, improperly cooked meat, mainly pork which I do not eat, tons of noodles and beans, and canned vegetables with little or no nutrients. Around the holidays, Thanksgiving and Christmas, the food is pretty decent but after that it's back to normal. Now the prison grows its own food. Sometimes, we eat fruits and vegetables from the fields, but most of the vegetables are bad. The good produce they sell. I know because I worked in the fields and the kitchen, so I know the politics. The only time I have access to fresh vegetables and fruit is when I have a visitor from the outside world and they are able to buy fresh fruits and small salads from the vending machines - at this time, I get a visit about once a month. It's not much but it's better than nothing. We also have a commissary that sells all kinds of food, really junk food, and processed meats. I have tried all of the meats, but I mostly eat tuna, mackerel and sardines. The fish is a little better, but my goal is to stop eating all animal flesh; those that fly, walk and swim. Think about it. The animals we are eating in the form of steaks, hot dogs, hamburgers, and chickens have been injected with all types of steroids, growth hormones and other chemicals. Then the poor animals are brutally slaughtered and cut up into bits and pieces and dressed up with preservatives, which is another name for embalming fluid to keep the meat from smelling and rotting inside the package. At the moment of slaughter, the animal is filled with terror and this energy is present when you finally sit down to eat the meat. Then we turn around and eat it and become sick. This is a destructive cycle we must break if we are serious about maintaining a healthy body.

Through my research and study, I have come to the conclusion that consumption of meat is bad for our health, and any honest doctor will tell you that meat is the cause of cancer and other diseases. The food we eat affects the mental and physical states, and wrong eating habits leads to disease in the body which affects the nervous system and other vital organs. When the body begins to ache and is in constant pain, it is hard for the individual to function and carry out his duties. So what we eat is very important.

The Bhagavad Gita, Chapter 17:7-10 describes the three classes of food and three classes of men. According to man's inherit nature, he is attracted to certain foods and rejects others.

Verse 7. Each of the three classes of men likes one of the three kinds of food; so also, their *yajnas,* penances and almsgivings. Hear thou about these distinctions.

Verse 8. Foods that promote longevity, vitality, endurance, health, cheerfulness, and good appetite; and that are savory, mild, substantial, and agreeable to the body, are liked by pure-minded (sattvic) persons.

Verse 9. Foods that are bitter, sour, salty, excessively hot, pungent, harsh and burning are preferred by overactive and nervous (rajasic) men and produce pain, sorrow and disease.

Verse 10. Goods that are nutritionally worthless, insipid, putrid, stale, refuse and impure are enjoyed by lazy and lethargic (tamasic) persons.

Sattvic (pure) foods include:

pomegranates, oranges, grapes, apples, bananas, mangoes, dates, honey, pears, plums, cantaloupe, cherries, figs, milk, rice, almonds, peanuts, sunflower seeds, lettuce, tomatoes, carrots, string beans, cabbage, cucumbers, green peas

Rajasic (stimulating) foods include:

spices, hot sauces, meats, eggs, fish, alcohol, salt, coffee, lemon, garlic, mustard

Tamasic (impure) foods include:

stale, raw meats, processed meats, spoiled fish, eggs, chicken, alcohol, tobacco, junk food, processed foods

As you can see, the food we eat is very important. Good foods equal good health, and bad foods equal bad health. When we become mindful of the foods we eat, we can determine our predominant nature. Most of us are a mixture of sattvic and rajasic. We swing back and forth like a pendulum. Also, there are some who are tamasic. Not only in the foods they eat, but their actions as well. It's like wolves in sheep's clothing - they may seem to be sattvic, but their actions are tamasic. Remember food is everything. You are what you eat.

The sages also tell us that it is very important to pay attention to chewing our food carefully. When we take big bites and swallow food without properly chewing it, the digestive system must work very hard to digest and assimilate the food as fuel for the body or waste. This robs you of your energy to do the things you want to do. But if we chew each bite so that the food becomes a paste in our mouths before swallowing, an amazing thing happens. There is an energy that is present in our saliva that enters the food and this goes with the food into our digestive system. The person who chews each bite of food into a paste has more energy, better digestion, a better complexion and a better frame of mind. Begin by practicing this for one meal a day. You'll see and experience the great difference it makes!

Why not adopt the yogic diet which is a truly healthy system to keep your mind alert and your body free of disease?

Questions for personal study:

1. What are the names of the two holy books that describe the yogic diet?
2. What are the three classes of food and men?
3. What are the sattvic foods?
4. What are the rajasic foods?
5. What are the tamasic foods?
6. What types of foods make up your daily diet?

Chapter 25 Yogic Exercise for the Mind, Body and Spirit

"A body that does no work is of no use, so you should make your body disciplined through regular work, *asanas*, *pranayama* and meditation.

- *Swami Muktananda*

The body is the temple of the living God, and we have been put in charge of it. There is nothing you can do on planet earth without the body. Therefore, we should take good care of it in the same way we would take care of the maintenance on our car.

This yogic exercise I would like to share with you is very beneficial, especially in today's unhealthy world. Hopefully after reading this chapter, you will try the exercises and make it a part of your life. This exercise is called *Surya Namaskar*, which means "the salutation to the sun". It consists of *asanas* (poses) and *pranayama* (controlled breathing). It prepares the mind for meditation. This exercise is commonly known as the *Sun Salutation*. The reason this exercise is called *Sun Salutation* is because it is done early in the morning, facing the rising sun. The sun is a symbol of God and has always been a source of life and health.

I practice the *Sun Salutation* three times weekly- Mondays, Wednesdays and Fridays. There are other yogic exercises that I practice, but the *Sun Salutation* is the best in that it works the entire body. This is a spiritual exercise that develops and strengthens the mind, body and spirit complex of Man. After one round of the Sun Salutation, my body is completely energized. The key is to keep the body in harmony through yogic exercise, a yogic diet and yogic thinking.

The benefits from this exercise are as follows: prevents disease, adds flexibility to the spine, increases circulation of blood throughout the body, reduces fat around the abdomen, stretches back muscles, joints, ligaments, tones up the nervous system, reduces stress and corrects improper breathing.

The *Sun Salutation* consists of twelve positions, making one full round of the exercise. The positions are outlined as follows. Most Hatha Yoga centers teach classes on the *Sun Salutation*.

You might want to go on YouTube and watch to see exactly how it is done before you begin. There are a few slight variations, but these are the basic poses. If you look carefully at the poses, you can see how each one benefits one or more parts of the body, for a total workout. As you perform each pose, you do so by breathing in and out in time with each posture. Start by doing five or more complete rounds each morning and work upwards from there. Over time , your body will become more limber and you will look just like the experts!

Keeping my body fit is very important to me in this environment that I live in. I don't have any fat on my body and I'm careful not to overeat. By keeping my body as healthy as I can, I can hold the strong and purifying energy of meditation. A healthy body can contain the powerful *kundalini shakti* energy that rises up the spine as one sits in meditation. In this way, I support my own spiritual journey by offering a healthy body to the divine power within me.

Questions for personal study:

1. The body is the temple of _____.
2. What does *surya namakar* mean?
3. The sun is the symbol of _____.
4. What are the benefits of the exercise?
5. How many positions are connected to this exercise?

Chapter 26 Yogic Thinking

"If men thought of God as much as they think of the world, who would not attain liberation?"

-Maitri Upanishads

The scriptures speak the truth. Liberation is only a thought away. If we truly believe in liberation, then our thoughts must be in harmony with our beliefs. Jesus said, "All things are possible for him who believes." Liberation is possible in this life time, only if we would think of God instead of the world. The world has become a spider web for most of us, and many people have become trapped by their own thoughts. Our thoughts play a very important part in our day to day lives. Our feelings, emotions, and moods are all connected to our thoughts. If we can control our thoughts, we can control our actions. The Bible says, "As a Man thinks in his heart, so is he. He (a yogi) is God, because of his thinking; therefore, he is liberated in God."

The thoughts of a yogi are supreme because his thoughts are one with the Guru, his spiritual guide and master. The yogi has become one with the Guru by meditating on the

Guru. By constantly meditating on the Guru's form and thinking of the Guru, our thoughts become pure. In the Guru Gita, Verse 20 it states, "Abandoning all thoughts of these - your stage in life, your caste, your reputation and increasing your well-being, think of nothing other than the Guru." The yogi abandons the ego thoughts of *I, me* and *mine*. He doesn't think to himself, "I've got this, I've got that, I have lots of money and a big house." By abandoning all of these worldly thoughts, the mind becomes free to think of the Guru.

The thoughts of a yogi play an important part in the mind, body, spirit complex of Man. Positive thoughts are healing, and negative thoughts are destructive. A yogi who thinks positive thoughts is able to purify his entire body, while negative thoughts are destructive causing dis-ease in the body. A yogi with positive thoughts purifies the atmosphere, and those around him, while negative thoughts of lust, anger and greed pollutes the atmosphere, and has an adverse affect on those around him. The atmosphere, believe it or not, is charged with all kinds of thoughts -happy thoughts and sad thoughts, thoughts of love, and thoughts of hate. Stress and depression are today's silent killers. Stress and depression are toxic thoughts that we entertain unconsciously every day. Yogic thinking allows us to tune out the lower thoughts and tune into the higher thoughts. Man is like a radio in that he is able to receive and transmit thought waves. The FM stands for *free mind*- free of toxic thoughts. The AM stands for *agitated mind* -chaotic, restless, doubting, worried and self-destructive. The tuning knob represents the yogi's ability to tune into the different states of consciousness. The Bible says in Colossians 3:2, "Set your mind on things above, not on things on the earth." The yogi sets his mind on the Guru, and nothing else. Meditation on the Guru is the highest form of worship.

Thoughts act in the same way as magnets, in that they attract. The law of attraction is about "like attracting like". People of similar thoughts are attracted towards each other. Charles Haanel, author of the "Master Key System" says, "The predominant thought or the mental attitude is the magnet and the law is that *like attracts like*, consequently, the mental attitude will invariably attract such conditions as correspond to its nature."

The threefold nature of man, *sattvic, rajas,* and *tamas* is reflected in the individual's thoughts, words, and actions. *Sattvic* and *tamas* are the two extremes on the same pole representing positive and negative. In the middle is *rajas*.

Rajas is like the balance between the two extremes, like most people they are stuck in the middle having to make a choice between *sattvic* and *tamas*. If a person has a strong will they can overcome their predominant nature. We have to be conscious at all times of our thoughts. Swami Sivananda said, "When some evil thought disturbs your mind, at once take to *padmasana* or *siddhasana* and do *pranayama* (yogic breathing), and the thought will leave you." Don't act on the thought, if you do, you will regret it in the end. We must remain calm in the midst of all thoughts that come and go, and the best way is through the practice of yogic thinking.

I'm sure that you can imagine that life here on Texas Death Row is filled with negative vibrations of the worst kind. Just because someone is incarcerated does not mean that their thoughts about themselves and others will change. And when you bring more than 200 such men into a very small space, the atmosphere becomes charged with a blanket of gloom and ill-feelings. But the light of God exists everywhere and the light is here on death row as well.

Imagine that you are an inmate on Death Row and you are walking with your hands and feet in chains to take a shower. You pass a man who wants to kill you and another man who wants to rape you and you are walking with a guard who is masochistic and likes to see people suffer. Suddenly you pass someone in a cell who is just simply watching you, with a look of love and compassion. That person doesn't say anything, but you feel the shift in the energy and you feel like maybe there is hope in this world after all. You know that, just as there is bad in this world, there is good as well and that you have a choice. Just in that single moment you feel uplifted.

This is what the life of a yogi is all about. Yes, we offer our spiritual practices because we want to stop our own inner pain and turmoil; we want to feel at peace. But when one person makes that effort, those vibrations go out into the world and touch others who are also searching for a way to happiness and peace. When you decide that you are going to turn your life around and make an consistent effort to know God, you change your environment as well. Believe it or not, your family and ancestors benefit from your practices. We are all connected.

Questions for personal study:

1. What happens when we make a decision to take control of our thoughts?
2. How does the yogi become one with the Guru?
3. What are the benefits of positive thinking?
4. What is the meaning of FM and AM?
5. What should you do when you become angry?

Chapter 27 *Pranayama*

"When the breath wanders, the mind is also unsteady, but when the breath is still, so is the mind and the yogis live long; therefore, one should hold the breath.

- *Hatha Yoga Pradipika*

What is the nature of the breath? In this teaching, we are going to look at pranayama, which is the science of breath, also commonly known as yogic breathing. *Pranayama* is a vast science that's been around for thousands of years. The word *pranayama* consists of two words - prana and yama. *Prana* means the *vital life force*, and yama means *self-control*. Pranayama is the control of *prana* or life force. All cultures around the world have a name for *prana*. In China it's called *chi*, in Japan it's called *ki* and in India it's called *prana*. In the Christian faith it's called the *Holy Spirit*. Prana is the universal life force of both the individual and the world. Prana is life itself, without prana we would cease to exist. Prana is also known as the *breath of life*, because life started with the breath. In the book of Genesis 2:7, it says, "And the Lord God formed man of the dust of the ground, and breathed into his nostrils the breath of life. And man became a living soul."

Through pranayama we are able to understand the power of the sacred breath. Jesus demonstrates this power of breath. In the Bible, John 20: 21-22.

21. So Jesus said to them again, "Peace to You! As the Father has sent me, I also send you."

22. And when He has said this, he breathed on them and said to them, "Receive the Holy Spirit."

The mind and prana are connected in that they act and react upon one another. The breath is the gross form of prana. In the *Yoga Vasishta*, the relationship between the mind and prana is described:

"O Rama! For the motion of the chariot, which is the physical body, God has created the mind and prana (vital breath), without which the body cannot function. When the prana departs, the mechanism of the body ceases and when the mind works, prana or vital breath moves. The relation between the mind and prana is like that between the driver and the chariot. Both exert motion one upon the other. Therefore, the wise should study regulation of prana or vital breath if they desire to suspend the restless activity of the mind and concentrate. The regulation of breath brings all happiness, material and spiritual, from the acquisition of kingdoms to supreme bliss. Therefore, O Rama! Study the science of breath."

Through pranayama, we are able to bring calmness to a restless mind. A calm mind like water reflects the image of God. A person who is able to keep Godly thoughts is God-conscious. Pranayama is key to keeping a calm mind. When a person becomes angry with someone he should pause, take a deep breath and allow his thoughts to settle down. The deep breath brings fresh oxygen to the brain and it allows the mind to release the anger. Some people say "calm down". In the scripture, Jesus said to the storm, "Peace be still". The storm represents the mind with its restless thoughts when the *prana* and *apana* become equalized, the mind becomes still. *Prana* is exhalation and *apana* is inhalation. There are the two vital breaths.

Through the practice of pranayama, the nadis are also purified. The nadis or nerves, are subtle channels in the human body that carry the vital life force. When the nadis are clogged up and full of impurities, the prana is unable to flow properly which is the cause of disease and other ailments. According to the

Yoga Shastras, there are 72 million nadis throughout the body. The three main nadis are *ida, pingala,* and *sushumna*. *Ida* flows through the left nostril and *pingala* through the right nostril. The ida nadi is symbolic of the moon breath, and the pingala nadi is symbolic of the sun breath. Ida is cooling and pingala is heating. The *sushumna* is the central nadi extending from the *muladhara chakra* at the base of the spine to the *sahasrara*, also known as the heavenly way or stairway to heaven. The sacred breath is one that comes from God. This breath becomes two when it enters the nostrils of man in the form of ida and pingala, the two breaths, becomes one again when it enters into the sushumna nadi, thus merging back into the original breath which is God. The goal of the yogi is to unite with the two breaths and make it flow up through the sushumna nadi. This is done through the practice on controlled breathing or pranayama.

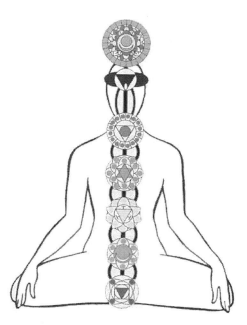

Take a moment to pause in your reading and take a deep breath. Focus on the in-breath and the out-breath. As you can see, we all practice pranayama consciously or unconsciously. Pranayama prepares the mind for concentration and meditation. It also helps in reducing stress and anger. Sometimes when a negative thought arises in my mind, I consciously take a deep breath, a positive breath and neutralize the negative thought. You can do it too!

For beginners, I recommend the breathing exercises below as described by *Shankara*. *Shankara* is the author of the *Crest Jewel of Discrimination*. He was one of the great poet saints of India. This exercise is very easy and healthy. Shankara says:

"The mind whose dross has been cleared away by pranayama becomes fixed in Brahman, therefore pranayama is taught. First, the nerves are to be purified; then comes the power to practice pranayama. Stopping the right nostril with the thumb, through the left nostril breathe in air, according to capacity; then, without any interval, expel the air through the right nostril, closing the left one. Again, inhaling through the right nostril, expel the air though the left, according to capacity. By practicing this at four periods of the day- before dawn, during midday, in the evening and at midnight, in fifteen days or a month, one may attain purity of the nerves."

This exercise is called alternate breathing. You can practice it standing up or sitting down. When the nerves become purified, the life-force will be able to flow freely throughout the body and within a month's time, you keep the practice up, you will see and feel the benefits of this exercise. This is the benefit of pranayama.

Keep in mind that the breath and the way that we breathe have a direct influence on our thoughts. You can feel the difference when you are feeling bad and you choose to pause, take a deep breath, allow your shoulders to open up and bring your head up. Look around you and as my Master says, "enjoy a transcendent view".

Questions for personal study:

1. What is pranayama?
2. Can we live without prana?
3. How do we calm the restless mind?
4. What are the three main nadis?
5. Where are the ida and the pingala nadis located?

Afterword

As you go through your life, remember that everything and everyone is connected. The thoughts in our mind lead us either to a life of love and peace or a life of stress and negative thinking. The choice is ours. This thinking impacts our bodies, our digestion and how we carry out our daily activities. When our state of being improves, our energy field changes and it co-mingles with all the energy fields around us and those energy fields are changed for the better. The small steps that we take to become more conscious of who we are and why we are here have an effect on everything and everyone around us. The world recognizes a "seeker" and whether I'm in here on Texas Death Row or out there on the streets, I've determined that I can make a difference in this world.

I've started my journey by working to heal the person inside. To do this, I have taken the aid of a genuine spiritual Master who has walked this path and completed the journey. A master of this kind is a rare gift to the world. Through my beloved Guru, I have received the spiritual awakening that will guide me the rest of my life, no matter where I am or what I've done in the past.

I'm not the only person who strives to walk steadfastly on the spiritual path in this place. Here on Death Row, there are Christians, Jews, Muslims, Buddhists, Catholics and all kinds of lovers of God. My guess is that we have a much higher percentage of people here who devoutly practice some kind of religion than you would find in the outside world.

The inmates who meditate and practice the yogic science on death row do so to keep their sanity. These conditions are inhumane and we all do the best we can to maintain a state where we can think positively and keep hope alive. Is it the hope that we will someday walk free? Well, maybe for some the answer is *yes*. But for the majority of us, we want to have the experience of God in our lives in every moment. We want to look around and see beauty in these walls and in these people with which we live. We want to experience freedom on the inside and by this, I mean inside these walls as well as inside our minds and hearts.

To find out more about Siddha Yoga and the Siddha lineage of divine Masters, you can visit http://www.siddhayoga.org

I would love to hear from you and learn about your spiritual experiences! You can write to me at:

Pete Russell, #999443

Polunsky Unit

3872 FM 350 South

Livingston, Texas 77351

USA

My wish for you on your spiritual journey is that you find a path in which you may experience the love and peace you are seeking. May that path lead you to know that, within your own being, you are God and that God permeates your life in every experience you have and in every person you meet. God is there in the good and in the bad.

Dear Reader, may you spend this lifetime coming ever closer to God and may you be a vehicle for good in this world. I love you.

Pete Russell, Texas Death Row Inmate

2013

Acknowledgements

I would like to sincerely thank all of those who have supported me through this writing process. Many thanks to Julie Muller for the typing and editing and also thanks to Joost Hogenboom for his great work and support in getting this book off the ground. Thanks to Gert Mampaey for his help as well. A special thanks to all of my brothers here on Texas Death Row for your encouragement. I could not have accomplished this without you.

My gratitude goes out to those spiritual masters who have walked the path before us and can guide us through the trials and tribulations of a life of steadfast devotion to God. As one writer said, it is the "road less travelled".

I have received much inspiration from all of the brothers and sisters that live on the inside of prison walls, carrying on a struggle for respect and humane conditions. And all of those on the outside who have fought for freedom and equality over the years here in the USA and around the world; your great work benefits us all.

Over the years I've received many visits from people who encouraged me to write about my experiences and discoveries as well as those visitors who encouraged me on the Siddha Yoga path. To all of you, I thank you with all of my heart.

Source Notes

My scriptural sources and quotes came from many different sources, some of which I no longer have access to because of the random practice of the confiscation and seizure of our possessions here on Texas Death Row.

Therefore, this book does not contain a bibliography on all of the resources that I utilized in my writing. All of the sources that I have quoted or mentioned in this book are, to my knowledge, widely available in different editions and I encourage you to seek them out and read them for yourself.